Puzzle Me the Right Answer to that One

Puzzle Me the Right Answer to that One

The Further Possibilities of Literature and Composition in an American High School

Volume 2

Joseph F. Riener

ROWMAN & LITTLEFIELD
Lanham • Boulder • New York • London

Published by Rowman & Littlefield

A wholly owned subsidiary of The Rowman & Littlefield Publishing Group, Inc.
4501 Forbes Boulevard, Suite 200, Lanham, Maryland 20706
www.rowman.com

Unit A, Whitacre Mews, 26-34 Stannary Street, London SE11 4AB, United Kingdom

British Library Cataloguing in Publication Information Available

Library of Congress Cataloging-in-Publication Data
Names: Riener, Joseph F., 1947-
Title: Puzzle me the right answer to that one : the further possibilities of literature and composition in an American high school / Joseph F. Riener.
Description: Lanham, Maryland : Rowman & Littlefield, [2015] | Includes index.
Identifiers: LCCN 2015026469| ISBN 9781475816976 (cloth : alk. paper) | ISBN 9781475816983 (pbk. : alk. paper) | ISBN 9781475816990 (electronic)
Subjects: LCSH: English language–Study and teaching (Secondary)–United States. | Literature–Study and teaching (Secondary)–United States.
Classification: LCC LB1631 .R5365 2015 | DDC 428.0071/2–dc23 LC record available at http://lccn.loc.gov/2015026469

∞™ The paper used in this publication meets the minimum requirements of American National Standard for Information Sciences—Permanence of Paper for Printed Library Materials, ANSI/NISO Z39.48-1992.

Printed in the United States of America

Thanks

To all my students, certainly. These volumes couldn't have happened without their participation over the many years.

To many parents of students. Their support allowed our coalition to work well.

To all the teachers I've had, both in the classroom and since then. I've aimed to imitate the good ones, avoid the mistakes of the others.

To all those friends who read over this manuscript and provided helpful commentary or encouragement: Mary Carpenter, Vivian Carroll, Tracy Hadden-Loh, Kate Winterkorn, Alan Burnce, Don Krumm, Stephanie Koenig, Art Siebens, Shane Achenbach, John Bailey, Alex Donahue and The Twenty First Century School Fund

To Robert Downey, who seems to bring good luck to every writer he knows. May he enjoy some for himself.

To Shannon Payne, whose questions inspire me.

To Rick Yorgey, Don and Louise Krumm, Ruth and Peter Nielsen-Jones, Bonnie and Randy Beers, Stephanie and George Koenig, Mary Filardo, Marlene Berlin, Jim Baller, and Bob Hoffman for their steadfast friendship and kindness over the years.

To Carole Huberman, who told me, "You'll land on your feet," at precisely the moment when everything about me was on the ground except my feet.

To Jesus Quintana, for his words of encouragement in a dark time.

To Sister Margarita, Pete, Jessica, and others, who showed me the door to other possibilities.

To Wilma Bonner and Steve Tarason, who permitted me to carve a niche.

To my children, Cedar, Alice, and Silas, and their pursuit of truth, justice, and beauty.

To Cathy Reilly, my love, my life, my muse, who kept saying, "Oh, honey, I think you should write this book."

to Cathy

Contents

Preface

I write for teachers, administrators, parents, as a record of one teacher's journey to find an effective educational voice. By my example, I aim to encourage others to find theirs. My stance, on the value of an individual teacher's perspective, stands in contrast to the notions of the Common Core Standards. To my mind, an independent educator embodies the freedom we value so highly in our democratic society.

I write for my former students, just in case they missed a class, or happened to be daydreaming, or didn't catch my drift the first time. I'm writing down all that I have said over the years.

I write for students I might have had, but geography, or time, or happenstance, prevented.

I write for my grandchildren, because I want them to know me and what I thought. I would like to be remembered for something more than my grandson's observation, "Grandpa, you swear a lot."

I want to explain myself to the other teachers at the school where I taught. As teacher evaluations became more fraught with issues of power and compliance, I became identified as the defiant one. I wouldn't alter my practice to please the evaluators. Others did. I became the pariah. I understand I was at a far different point in my life. With children grown, college checks all written, and a small mortgage, I could afford to challenge the "school reformers." And somehow it was in my Swiss and Irish blood to take on this role.

I respect all those who did what they had to do to survive in the classroom given our political vulnerability. This book stands as a tribute to them as fellow travelers, those who shifted and endured what they had to, to keep working with young people.

And this:

> They think math's a young man's game. Speed keeps them racing, makes them feel sharp. There's this fear that your creativity peaks around twenty-three and it's all downhill from there. Once you hit fifty it's over, you might as well teach high school.
>
> From the Tony Award-winning play *Proof*, by David Auburn [the character, Hal, a math professor, is talking about why math profs take speed].

This book attempts to show that real intellectual work, of thinking, of reading, of getting at the meaning of a poem, a short story, a novel, may happen in high school.

It serves to offer the best argument I can make against those who insist that teaching resides in form. This book devotes itself to content. I talk about students' writing assignments, works of literature and nonfiction, Big Ideas.

Like Cervantes, and tons of old geezer politicians and movie stars and baseball players, I'm writing as I arrive at the end of things and have some stories. Your edification or entertainment at reading becomes a by-product of my enjoyment in the telling.

The University of Virginia professor Siva Vaidhyanathan talks of the classroom as a sacred space. In reading this book, I hope you believe I honored that notion.

For years I told my students, "No matter what happens to you in life, you can always write about it." Here goes.

Introduction

This is a book, divided into two volumes, about teaching Advanced Placement English classes at an urban high school with a diverse population. Volume One presents the class offered to juniors, and Volume Two, the one to seniors. These two classes, which in previous times might have been termed honor classes, now have a link to a nationwide exam. Some AP subjects, like AP History or AP Chemistry, have a set curriculum, or a body of knowledge that the exam tests. In contrast, both AP English exams, "Grammar and Composition" and "Literature and Composition," measure skills. There are no set curriculums for either AP English exam.

Both volumes represent possible AP English curriculums. They have elements of old-style *civics* in them. They concern themselves with how students understand their place in the world, how as young people they might develop their consciousness as either American or world citizens. Both volumes hold to the premise that literature exists for teachers and students to use as tools for such conversations and potential insights.

Reading everything straight through, from Volume One to Volume Two, would give the reader a sense of the rhythm and development of ideas as they unfolded throughout the courses. Perhaps picking and nibbling, seeing what's said about Holden or Huck, Hamlet or Beowulf, Stanley Kunitz or Seamus Heaney, might induce the reader to invest more time in the volumes.

Teachers of writing for young people might want to start with the comments about student essays interspersed throughout both volumes. The Appendices might be interesting to readers who like finding out things about someone by taking a tour of their attic, garage, or basement.

The volumes are for teachers who have students willing to do homework as preparation for college work. At the high school where these courses were presented, AP English students distinguished themselves from other students mainly by their assent to more homework. There weren't entry barriers like grade point averages or prior knowledge to exclude students. If they were up for the challenge, all students were welcome.

Readers who work their way through both volumes will see that there are some elements of greater complexity and depth in the course offered to seniors. They're older. They are more able to take in the moral challenges and tears that literature offers. The curriculum choices, in texts and treatment, reflect this age difference.

As happens at many schools with a similar diverse urban population, many of the students were of European-American background. The students of color in the AP classes were largely middle class. Few poor minority students came to AP classes, mine or any others, despite our open-door policy, or persistent urging.

These volumes aim to be useful to teachers of students that are looking forward to college and willing to engage with what was assigned. As much as anyone can make such a claim, these students weren't all that different from most young people in our country today. Perhaps they were more secular, more cosmopolitan than most, given the context of going to school in a large city. They were students who had a sense of an academic future. What is offered in both volumes claims to be useful for all of them.

For those who teach the most ambitious students, striving for admission to highly selective colleges, these two volumes, by offering a large amount of reading and striving for depth of inquiry and understanding, help to prepare those students for what lies ahead.

Offered here are poems, short stories, plays, novels, why they were chosen, what might be said about them to students to deepen their understanding of literature. There's no argument presented that the works themselves are an integral part of what human beings need to know to get through life or even consider themselves educated persons. These texts are mediums, ways of saying something, drawing attention to an idea, a concept, a way of seeing the world.

These volumes attempt to inspire rather than prescribe what ought to occur in a high school classroom.

Readers might adapt the discussion of the literature offered here as they see fit. The volumes will hopefully be useful to those devising their own way of being in a classroom. They demonstrate what may happen with young people within such confines.

Many people claim they never had a good literature teacher, at high school or college. These volumes might be useful to such readers as a way to involve themselves more deeply with literature. Twain, Shakespeare, Hurston, Camus, Beowulf, Frankenstein, Quixote, and all the rest wait on the shelves for that moment in a life when they may come alive as objects of amazement and wonder. These volumes might serve as their midwife.

Chapter 1

The First Classes for Seniors

THIS

by Czeslaw Milosz

If I could at last tell you what is in me,
if I could shout: people! I have lied by pretending it was not there.
It was there, day and night.

Only thus was I able to describe your inflammable cities,
Brief loves, games disintegrating into dust,
earrings, a strap falling lightly from a shoulder,
scenes in bedrooms and on battlefields.

Writing has been for me a protective strategy
Of erasing traces. No one likes
A man who reaches for the forbidden.

I asked help of rivers in which I used to swim, lakes
With a footbridge over the rushes, a valley
Where an echo of singing had twilight for its companion.
And I confess my ecstatic praise of being
Might just have been exercises in the high style.
Underneath was this, which I do not attempt to name.

This. Which is like the thoughts of a homeless man walking in an alien
city in freezing weather.
And like the moment when a tracked-down Jew glimpses the heavy
helmets of the German police approaching.

The moment when the crown prince goes for the first time down to the city and sees the truth of the world: misery, sickness, age, and death.

Or the immobile face of someone who has just understood that he's been abandoned forever.

Or the irrevocable verdict of the doctor.

This. Which signifies knocking against a stone wall and knowing that the wall will not yield to any imploration.

******

WOMEN AND HORSES

by Maxine Kumin

After Auschwitz, to write a poem is barbaric

Theodor Adorno

After Auschwitz: after ten of my father's kin–
the ones who stayed–starved, then were gassed in the
    camps.
After Vietnam, after Korea, Kuwait, Somalia, Haiti,
    Afghanistan.
After the Towers. This late in the life of our haplessly orbiting
    world
let us celebrate whatever scraps the muse, that naked child,
can pluck from the still smoldering dumps.

If there's a lyre around, strike it! A body, stand back, give it
    air!
Let us have sparrows laying their eggs in bluebird boxes.
Let us have bluebirds insouciantly nesting elsewhere.
Lend us navel-bared teens, eyebrow- and nose ringed
    prodigies
crumbling breakfast bagels over dogeared and jelly-smeared
    texts.
Allow the able-bodied among us to have steamy sex.

Let there be fat old ladies in flowery tent dresses at bridge
    tables.
Howling babies in dirty diapers and babies serenely at rest.

War and detente will go on, detente and renewed tearings
   asunder,
we can never break free from the dark and degrading past.
Let us see life again, nevertheless, in the words of Isaac Babel
as a meadow over which women and horses wander.

As with the junior year, the course starts with poems. There's no analysis offered, just these word-sounds, to set a tone, establish a way of listening in the class. It may be a little strange, particularly for students who didn't have the junior course. That's okay. Strange is good. Allows for an expansion of the boundaries of what might be able to happen in the room.

This class does push. Both of these poems announce this. The students will have a long look at human-caused horror. That's where so much literature comes from. The course uses some analytical tools from moral philosophy and psychology to try to understand why humans have been so terrible toward each other. This effort intends for students to craft an authentic hope to live their lives with. Certainly some poets and writers have found it, as have Holocaust and Rwandan genocide survivors. It may not go very far with my American young people, living in such peace and comfort, as they begin their lifelong journeys to reconcile the ways of man to man. But this is the road all educated people ought to be on.

It's a class about literature from Over There. Mainly the British Isles, but also continental Europe, both contemporary and a few ancients. Since Toni Morrison's *Beloved*, both in theme and substance, might be considered more similar to the Russians than Updike or even Faulkner, this senior-year course reads her novel *despite* its seemingly American roots. Students will consider murderers of kings, of children, of friends, of masses of human beings. These portrayals evoke the fundamental moral and psychological questions, which is why Sophocles and Shakespeare and Dickens and Wilde and Morrison find them so compelling.

The various essays and poems of the course consider how humankind might respond to war and human suffering. The literature isn't offered as a guideline of how students ought to live. The attempt becomes curatorial. Exposure to these writings will help students see how others thought and acted when they confronted *the truth of the world.*

The course also presents, as an object of study, an astounding change in human consciousness, occurring at this precise moment in history. In the views of most heterosexual people, gay people have gone from the state of being pariahs, hounded or shunned or tortured or executed, to a tolerance and acceptance Oscar Wilde or Harvey Milk could hardly have dreamt about. This class seeks to raise some questions, through some literary art and essays, that seek to dramatize this particular form of oppression, which might help students understand how it now is on its way to being overcome.

This course faces a practical difficulty. By February seniors understand that their relation with school and grades fundamentally changes. College applications don't consider second-semester senior grades. Students thus experience a precipitous drop in their desire for good grades. Teachers find themselves no longer the mighty Givers of Grades. Going forward from February to May depends solely on students' desire to learn. This is not a negligible motivation, but it needs to be managed.

Senioritis arises from the environmental pollutant promulgated by the scheduling requirements of University Factories. Students have to delay their adolescence as they plunge into the Academic Mines of sixteen-hour days in order to become Successful Applicants. Such sacrifices render them helpless against the tide of frivolity and romance this hiatus offers them. The course packs as much as possible into the September-through-February months.

After that, the course focuses on short, but high-interest, texts, like *Frankenstein, Beowulf,* and brief selections from *Don Quixote* and *Canterbury Tales.* Students can find the energy to offer one last summing-up essay in May. They work hard that first semester, since they want to show something good to their colleges. In the second semester, the course resembles a nice, friendly book group until graduation.

Over the years, these young people have demonstrated much maturity at contending with Milosz's *this* that the course presents. They really do think about it, write about it, seem to be different people at the end of it. That's the plan.

SOME POEMS BY SEAMUS HEANEY

OYSTERS

Our shells clacked on the plates.
My tongue was a filling estuary,
My palate hung with starlight:
As I tasted the salty Pleiades
Orion dipped his foot into the water.

Alive and violated,
They lay on their bed of ice:
Bivalves: the split bulb
And philandering sigh of ocean
Millions of them ripped and shucked and scattered.

We had driven to that coast
Through flowers and limestone
And there we were, toasting friendship,
Laying down a perfect memory
In the cool of thatch and crockery.

Over the Alps, packed deep in hay and snow,
The Romans hauled their oysters south to Rome:
I saw damp panniers disgorge
The frond-lipped, brine-stung
Glut of privilege
And was angry that my trust could not repose
In the clear light, like poetry or freedom
Leaning in from sea. I ate the day
Deliberately, that its tang
Might quicken me all into verb, pure verb.

Imagine someone at a restaurant, having a great time with friends or family. Out on the street, this person notices a homeless old woman pushing a cart, rummaging through the trash can on the corner, then eating something she finds there. Might change the taste of the restaurant food, even the atmosphere of the entire evening.

The class spends a fair amount of time with this poem. It encapsulates much of the moral dilemma students confront in the world. People in the wealthy Western world are having such a good time. They know little of war and misery, particularly the urban guerilla sort of Heaney's Northern Ireland during "The Troubles." Students read of the suffering going on elsewhere, or at other times. The media offer many photographs of *millions of them ripped and shucked and scattered.*

This disrupts *friendship,* disturbs *perfect memory.* Americans and those the military protects are, after all, the new *Romans.* The most lethal military in history protects this life. A terrible day in Boston is a light day in Baghdad, Damascus, Kabul, Aleppo, to offer the most recent juxtapositions, or in Beirut, Sarajevo, Darfur, Kigali, to go back only a few years. Not sharing this misery becomes a *privilege* shared by many in the industrialized world. When such people can't maintain their *repose,* like contemplating *poetry or freedom* might do, it makes them *angry.*

What to do? How should people of *privilege* respond, when they see suffering?

Many insulate themselves in the pleasant world. This poet doesn't. He resolves to *eat the day deliberately.* He will stay aware of his happy life, in juxtaposition with the world's misery. He will use that *tang* to *quicken him into verb, pure verb.* It calls him to action, to make him a better poet.

This becomes the continual friction, or *tang* as the poet terms it, in this class. The effort students will need to make involves an understanding of how they might *quicken* themselves in response to what they see and feel and learn about the world.

REQUIEM FOR THE CROPPIES

The pockets of our greatcoats full of barley—
No kitchens on the run, no striking camp—
We moved quick and sudden in our own country.
The priest lay behind ditches with the tramp.
A people hardly marching—on the hike—
We found new tactics happening each day:
We'd cut through reins and rider with the pike
And stampede cattle into infantry,
Then retreat through hedges where cavalry must be thrown.
Until, on Vinegar Hill, the final conclave.
Terraced thousands died, shaking scythes at cannon.
The hillside blushed, soaked in our broken wave.
They buried us without shroud or coffin
And in August the barley grew up out of the grave.

Many of Heaney's poems arise out of Irish history. This one is about the Irish rebels in the late eighteenth century who tried to overthrow British rule. Too bad for them that they were so close to Britain, unlike the North American colonists who had recently achieved their independence. "Losing America" made the Brits doubly determined not to get whipped by the less-than-human Irish, a couple of days' sailing time away.

Although the rebels, united across class and religion, and nicknamed "croppies" because of haircuts in imitation of participants in the French Revolution, enjoyed some initial success, they couldn't withstand the assault of Britain's heavy artillery. Surrounded, many wanting to surrender, the rebels died as the British bombed and bombed their stronghold of Vinegar Hill, *shaking scythes at cannon.* Britain made sure, in its nineteenth-century policy toward Ireland, to reward the Protestants, even colonize Northern Ireland, to keep the Irish people divided. But those seeds of freedom sprouted anew in the twentieth century, as new rebels fought and won freedom for most of Ireland.

This, then, becomes a poem of hope for all those *buried without shroud or coffin.* Their graves were not the end, but rather the opportunity for vitality to spring from this soil. Americans might think of the freed slaves who fought and died for the Union forces in the Civil War, or even of the Civil Rights-era people who were killed and buried in unmarked graves. Much sprang from the soil of their sacrifice.

CASUALTY

I

He would drink by himself
And raise a weathered thumb
Towards the high shelf,
Calling another rum
And blackcurrant, without
Having to raise his voice,
Or order a quick stout
By a lifting of the eyes
And a discreet dumb-show
Of pulling off the top;
At closing time would go
In waders and peaked cap
Into the showery dark,
A dole-kept breadwinner
But a natural for work.
I loved his whole manner,
Sure-footed but too sly,
His deadpan sidling tact,
His fisherman's quick eye
And turned observant back.

Incomprehensible
To him, my other life.
Sometimes on the high stool,
Too busy with his knife
At a tobacco plug
And not meeting my eye,
In the pause after a slug
He mentioned poetry.
We would be on our own
And, always politic
And shy of condescension,
I would manage by some trick
To switch the talk to eels
Or lore of the horse and cart
Or the Provisionals.

But my tentative art
His turned back watches too:
He was blown to bits
Out drinking in a curfew
Others obeyed, three nights

After they shot dead
The thirteen men in Derry.
PARAS THIRTEEN, the walls said,
BOGSIDE NIL. That Wednesday
Everyone held
His breath and trembled.

II

It was a day of cold
Raw silence, wind-blown
Surplice and soutane:
Rained-on, flower-laden
Coffin after coffin
Seemed to float from the door
Of the packed cathedral
Like blossoms on slow water.
The common funeral
Unrolled its swaddling band,
Lapping, tightening
Till we were braced and bound
Like brothers in a ring.

But he would not be held
At home by his own crowd
Whatever threats were phoned,
Whatever black flags waved.
I see him as he turned
In that bombed offending place,
Remorse fused with terror
In his still knowable face,
His cornered outfaced stare
Blinding in the flash.

He had gone miles away
For he drank like a fish
Nightly, naturally
Swimming towards the lure
Of warm lit-up places,
The blurred mesh and murmur
Drifting among glasses
In the gregarious smoke.
How culpable was he
That last night when he broke
Our tribe's complicity?
'Now, you're supposed to be

An educated man,'
I hear him say. 'Puzzle me
The right answer to that one.'

III

I missed his funeral,
Those quiet walkers
And sideways talkers
Shoaling out of his lane
To the respectable
Purring of the hearse . . .
They move in equal pace
With the habitual
Slow consolation
Of a dawdling engine,
The line lifted, hand
Over fist, cold sunshine
On the water, the land
Banked under fog: that morning
I was taken in his boat,
The screw purling, turning
Indolent fathoms white,
I tasted freedom with him.
To get out early, haul
Steadily off the bottom,
Dispraise the catch, and smile
As you find a rhythm
Working you, slow mile by mile,
Into your proper haunt
Somewhere, well out, beyond . . .

Dawn-sniffing revenant,
Plodder through midnight rain,
Question me again.

"The Troubles" was a largely urban civil war in Northern Ireland, between the Catholic minority and the Protestant majority, in that part of Ireland still part of the United Kingdom, from the late 1960s through the 1990s. There were bombings in bars, assassinations of government officials and rebels, shooting of unarmed demonstrators. The violence spread from Northern Ireland to The Republic of Ireland, and to Britain itself. "The Troubles" was a prototype of many violent conflicts around the world, from insurgencies in Iraq, or Chechnya, or in Israeli-occupied Palestine.

Such conflict is very close, very personal, very cruel. Heaney's poetry, reflecting on his experiences living in Northern Ireland, emerges quite sadly as universal in the contemporary world.

Heaney worked at a bar when he went to university. There he met this old fisherman. Students may have already met people, in their summer jobs or travels, who are outside their academic world. Sometimes, as for Heaney, these people can be quite compelling. They can possess a wisdom, or at least a view of the world and work, quite distinct from that put forth in our books and philosophies.

Heaney's fisherman defied the curfew imposed by the rebels, the Irish Republican Army, on an area in the city of Derry in Northern Ireland that they controlled, called Bogside. The British Paramilitary Forces, the *Paras*, had shot dead thirteen demonstrators. *Everybody held their breath and trembled* because the IRA was certain to retaliate. They set a bomb in the very bar the fisherman went to. *How culpable was he that last night when he broke our tribe's complicity?* Did this man deserve his fate? He wasn't about to obey those whom some termed "freedom fighters" and others termed "terrorists." *Now you're supposed to be an educated man . . . puzzle me the right answer to that one.*

He's asking if people are innocent if they ignore the conflicts in the world, and go on their way. Certainly the Boston bombers, the 9/11 hijackers, thought their targets were worthy. They wished to bring some of the pain of their lives, or their history, to privileged people. They certainly succeeded in that effort. Heaney wishes to question, in the violent death of his beloved fisherman, what is the scale of innocence, or of culpability, in any of these actions. No moral question is more powerful than this one in our contemporary lives.

FROM THE REPUBLIC OF CONSCIENCE

I

When I landed in the republic of conscience
it was so noiseless when the engines stopped
I could hear a curlew high above the runway.
At immigration, the clerk was an old man
who produced a wallet from his homespun coat
and showed me a photograph of my grandfather.
The woman in customs asked me to declare
the words of our traditional cures and charms
to heal dumbness and avert the evil eye.
No porters. No interpreter. No taxi.
You carried your own burden and very soon
your symptoms of creeping privilege disappeared.

II

Fog is a dreaded omen there but lightning
spells universal good and parents hang
swaddled infants in trees during thunderstorms.
Salt is their precious mineral. And seashells
are held to the ear during births and funerals.
The base of all inks and pigments is seawater.
Their sacred symbol is a stylized boat.
The sail is an ear, the mast a sloping pen,
the hull a mouth-shape, the keel an open eye.
At their inauguration, public leaders
must swear to uphold unwritten law and weep
to atone for their presumption to hold office—
and to affirm their faith that all life sprang
from salt in tears which the sky-god wept
after he dreamt his solitude was endless.

III

I came back from that frugal republic
with my two arms the one length, the customs
woman having insisted my allowance was myself.
The old man rose and gazed into my face
and said that was official recognition
that I was now a dual citizen.
He therefore desired me when I got home
to consider myself a representative
and to speak on their behalf in my own tongue.
Their embassies, he said, were everywhere
but operated independently
and no ambassador would ever be relieved.

This is a difficult poem for students. It's pretty bewildering at first. Takes a while to have its meaning emerge. It's well worth it, given that it is one of Heaney's most celebrated and referenced poems, serving as an anthem for the human-rights group Amnesty International.

He conjures up a geographical and political place where a moral center prevails. He's using *conscience* both in the sense Amnesty uses the phrase "prisoners of conscience," meaning people arrested for their political protest activities, or for breaking laws that violate human rights, and in the more general sense of the location of the individual moral understanding of the world. Not many people visit, as he indicates the airport isn't very busy. When his plane stops, he can hear a bird chirping.

His grandfather knew the place. The woman in customs sought out ways to have people listen, and avoid evil. Some of the students, who have traveled to poor foreign places might resonate already with the lines, *No porters. No interpreter. No taxi. You carried your own burden and very soon your symptoms of creeping privilege disappeared.* This references back to the use of *privilege* in the poem "Oysters," a powerful notion that expresses separation from the world of many people in the Western world. Here in the Republic, it disappears, so that the traveler sees what there is to see.

In this place, *fog* as in "the fog of war," is dreaded, because it means people can't see clearly. That's why lighting, since it dispels the darkness, is desired, even by the very young. *Salt,* as in "take that with a pinch of salt," or skepticism, is highly valued. *Seashells,* with the sound of eternity, connect with the humans' comings and goings. All written words are involved with this skepticism, embodied in the salt water. Their *sacred symbol* expresses the value of seeing, hearing, telling, the values of a free press that are crucial to a morality of public policy. Public leaders, recognizing their huge power, must be humble. They must understand that what unites all living beings, even their deity, is *loneliness.*

He returns from that place, with his body in proportion, his sense of himself validated. He was now a *dual citizen*, charged with speaking on behalf of his own conscience, *in my own tongue.* The burden, or the opportunity, would be his for the rest of his life. *No ambassador would ever be relieved.*

This poem celebrates the power of the idea of human rights, and how organizations such as Amnesty International implement this idea. They petition, they pester, they research, they encourage people of conscience to continue working on behalf of justice and human values. This movement, growing out of the horrors of the twentieth century, finds its poetic expression in Heaney's verse. These four poems serve as an appropriate introduction to a central theme of this course.

Chapter 2

"What Are You Going to Do with That?"

Readings: "What Are You Going to Do with That?" by Mark Danner, and "If We Fail to Act" by Paul Farmer.

This class promotes the values of a liberal education. It wishes students to become people of conscience. Two powerful pieces evoke this notion.

Mark Danner, a journalism professor at UC Berkeley and Bard College, spoke to recent graduates who had majored in English, which he envisions as learning to become a humanist:

> that is, [this] means not only to see clearly the surface of things and to see beyond those surfaces, but to place oneself in opposition, however subtle, an opposition that society seldom lets you forget . . . and whatever [students] they decide to do with "that," they see developing the moral imagination as more important than securing economic self-justification. (From *The New York Review of Books*, June 23, 2005)

Danner talks of contemporary history, and how being able to read well leaves people as outsiders, in opposition to the government, or the society, and its lies:

> after September 11 . . . our government decided to change this country from a nation that officially does not torture to one, officially, that does. What is interesting about this fact is not that it is hidden but that it is revealed. We know this or rather those who are willing to read know it . . . . And we, as I have said, remain fairly few.

He quotes, at the end of his speech, another poem by Czeslaw Milosz, about being present at the end of a world, in Warsaw, 1944, as the Nazis destroyed the city and its insurgent inhabitants. In the poem, Danner wishes his listeners to see that:

> And now, as then, truth does matter. Integrity—much rarer than talent or brilliance—does matter . . . . I hope you will remember your own questioning spirit.

Danner's speech helps connect ideas in literature with engagement in the world. Rather than viewing English majors, or those who pursue a liberal education, as separate from the ways of the world, Danner places such people at the vital center, as those who see and speak from their conscience. For students to view their education this way allows for the possibility of their doing important work in the world.

Paul Farmer's essay, from *Notre Dame Magazine*, Autumn 2006, stressed the centrality of the right to health care for the world's poor. He declares it to be crucial to any true understanding of human rights. Many advocate for civil and political rights as distinct from social and economic ones. Farmer terms overcoming this division as "the most pressing human-rights problem of our time."

As long as mainstream human-rights organizations do not understand how poverty and inequality are also human-rights violations, rather than simply distracting background consideration, there is little hope of advancing the case for social and economic rights.

Farmer believes it will not be sufficient for the poor to receive pity or virtuous aid. Health care ought to be a right, not a commodity that is available for purchase.

He talks of the history of Haiti, where he has labored to establish a health clinic. The country was treated as a pariah after its successful slave rebellion against the French at the beginning of the nineteenth century. Despite its condemnation of slavery then and its embrace of modern notions of human rights, it has been impoverished because it threatened American society's values in both centuries. Haiti is now the poorest country in the Western Hemisphere, with the highest rate of HIV infection. If all this is to change, in very poor countries like Haiti or Rwanda, it will require rich countries to accept their obligation to provide health care, not merely as a matter of compassion, but as what is due to any human being.

Farmer offers the Haitian phrase, *tout moun se moun* (we are all human beings) as a way to express the solidarity people ought to feel with the poor in the world.

In Haiti, Rwanda, and even Boston, service to the destitute sick reveals the sharp limitations of what can be done to allay misery without a broad understanding of why some people have so little while others enjoy a peculiarly modern surfeit.

He challenges his Catholic readers to go beyond merely performing works of mercy. He'd rather that they insisted that true feelings for fellow humans imply extending the benefits of modern medical care to everyone.

With both Danner and Farmer's ideas, there isn't much offered in class by way of analysis or even explanation. Some of the background of historical references they make in their pieces might get filled in. There's some discussion of the difficult questions like "Are you open to understanding the obligation that your privilege places on you, towards the world's poor?" Or, "What should we do with our current policy of executing human beings with drones, without trial?" But the purpose is mainly to expose students to ideas about human rights from thinkers whose working lives incorporate these ideas. It's fine if the class conversation doesn't go very far. These ideas are fraught for my young students, evoking their relationship to their family and their nation, and the values of both. It may take years for them to understand, let alone have language for, what they think and feel. This is preparation for a long inquiry. By the time they have something to say, they may have even forgotten these specific essays, just as a classical musicians can't recall the first time they heard Bach's unaccompanied cello suites.

Chapter 3

Sex, Drugs, Rock and Roll
in Ancient Greece

Reading: *The Bacchae* by Euripides, translated by David Greig.

Human rights is only one theme of the course. It also intends to make sure students connect to the literature of the world. Their education ought to involve the understanding that human beings have thought and felt in ways these young people now experience for the first time. With this knowledge, students can then mock those who find fault with *kids these days*, their sexuality and drugs and music. From the beginning of humans making art, artists have portrayed the power of the erotic, the narcotic, and oh, those drums.

Typically, the course has students read the assigned work first, and then some understanding of it gets provided in class discussions. But this play, on the page, wouldn't have been intelligible or held their interest if it hadn't been mediated initially by some interpretation. Students said they appreciated this. It helped them enjoy, even laugh at the play, in both its comedic absurdity and tragic horror.

They read the following essay before the play:

How students should read *The Bacchae*:

This is a tale of sex, drugs and rock and roll. Or, actually, s, d, r&r is the tale of Dionysus.

He's an ancient Greek god, not a human being. He doesn't care about mercy, justice, human suffering, or share in any commonality with us. He wants to be honored. Consider him a force of nature, a hurricane, an earthquake, leukemia. He doesn't even have gender. He assumes one, sort of, so as not to confuse humans too much.

Remember, the play arises out of a pre-Christian (by 500 years) imagination. Dionysus embodies attributes now seen in the figure of the devil: shape-shifting, deception, temptation to ensnare humans. He's not Apollo or Jesus. He's no hero.

When Freud wanted to label his mother/son concept, he grabbed the name of a character from this imaginative world (the Oedipus complex). Greek mythology isn't so much a religious system as it is a psychological one.

Dionysus is the god of wine. Poor ancient Greeks, that beverage was the only way they knew how to get high. The awesome Thai weed, let alone poppy-flower cultivation, haven't yet become part of the culture. Think of Dionysus' devotees, the Bacchae, or Maenads, as you might any group of hard-core stoners or junkies. They get intoxicated, sing, dance, have lots o' sex. It's all very compelling to the participants, don't you know?

See Pentheus as in charge of the War on Drugs. He intends to wipe out Dionysus and his groupies. He doesn't want to acknowledge the power that these mind-altering drugs have over mere humans, or reach some accommodation with this power.

Connect Pentheus' determination to his sexism. He doesn't want women to find other life activities besides laboring for men. He derides women for their sexuality. The play is his tragedy, stemming from these flaws.

Evoš is the word Euripides used. This translation uses *scream*. The Bacchae refer to Dionysus as The Scream. Think of the reception a rock star receives, bounding on stage. Also think of Edvard Munch's *The Scream*. It's what people do, when filled with more emotion than words can contain.

Some attribute to Dionysus the beginning of tragedy, since he's the god of imagination, arising out of these altered states. Enjoy how much our pleasure and struggle over s, d, r&r go back 2500 years. Pentheus, the human, is so confined, blind.

Dionysus is so charming, interesting.

Party on.

Chapter 4

The Struggles of a Survivor

Reading: *Great Expectations* by Charles Dickens.

The course hopes to convey how wonderful a storyteller Charles Dickens still proves to be. He wrote enough that they might take a lifetime reading it all. His collected works might even be considered a consolation of aging. He's so funny and sweet, possessing such a keen eye for human suffering, particularly in a world without a social safety net. His characters live in the imagination. Pip, Joe, Mrs. Joe, Jaggers, Miss Havisham, Estella, Magwitch, Wemmick enrich the readers' lives.

Consider just a few snippets, almost throwaway lines, as illustrations. In describing two characters leaving a pub, Dickens tells us,

> The sergeant took a polite leave of the ladies, and parted from Mr. Pumblechook as from a comrade; though I doubt if he were quite as fully sensible of that gentleman's merits under arid conditions, as when something moist was going. (pp. 33–34)

When Pip first comes into his money, he gets measured for a gentleman's suit at the town's tailor's shop. The shop assistant collapses in awe when he sees his former fellow poor child,

> and my first decided experience of the stupendous power of money, was, that it had morally laid upon his back, Trabb's boy. (p. 152)

In the scene of family madness with Herbert Pocket's family, Mr. Pocket, exasperated with his wife's negligence of their infant, exclaims,

"Good God! . . . Are infants to be nutcrackered into their tombs, and is nobody to save them?" (p. 194)

We have the delight of Wemmick, leading Pip to the church, then saying,

"Halloa! . . . Here's Miss Skiffins! Let's have a wedding!" (p. 453)

Dickens portrays a world long gone in the prosperous portion of it, but still present in Bangladesh or Nigeria or Mexico. He shows how cruel people can be to each other, because of the lack of institutional structures to protect the weak, the orphaned, the sick. Dickens fully used his storytelling art to reveal this world so that modern societies might do away with it, as Bangladeshi and Nigerian and Mexican storytellers are attempting to do in their countries. Humanity wishes them as much success as Dickens has enjoyed.

Beyond the pleasure at this story of a young man growing up, how can Pip be understood? There's a tone of regret in the story of his early life that he's telling us, from some point later in his life. He blames himself. He expresses much remorse for how he thought and felt, particularly towards Joe. But should he? Joe certainly didn't seem to feel bitter towards Pip. When he felt condescended to or uncomfortable, Joe took care of himself.

Joe was a good father. He understood that those they raise need some distance or some allowance as they grow up. The young will push away those who cared for them to establish their own lives. Pip seemed to feel worse about how he treated Joe than Joe ever did.

Should readers share Pip's sense that becoming a gentleman was a foolish endeavor? Many poor young people dream that dream, of riches, respect, getting the girl. It reflects their growing awareness of much poverty and lack of status. Once they achieve a life and love, almost all grow out of it. They might feel some ruefulness at their dreams, later in life, but Pip offers a fairly severe self-criticism, a tone, particularly at the end of the book, of much remorse for his actions.

Yet, readers see this young person treated badly by Mrs. Joe, Miss Havisham, Estella. Pip's great affection for Estella and Magwitch becomes clear. Pip may have felt ashamed of his initial repulsion at the scruffy old codger who proved to be his benefactor, but Magwitch didn't. The escaped convict felt so well treated by Pip's initial help that he gave Pip a fortune. Magwitch, if readers could talk to him in the Heaven that all good Dickens characters go to when they die, would surely relate that he had quite a good death given his life and status as a prisoner awaiting execution. Someone loving him, holding his hand as he slips off, why, that's far more than Magwitch dreamed was possible for himself.

It isn't regret Pip is experiencing, but something much deeper and more abiding. His devotion and sacrifice to those two misbegotten characters, Estella and Magwitch, seem exemplary, but melancholy pervades his tale.

How might this grief, for that's what his deep sadness suggests, be understood?

Consider the opening scene. Pip's an orphan, except for his older sister. He survived some illness or another that regularly took away whole families in those days. For Pip's family, mom and dad, and five siblings are buried in the graveyard. Much is now known about the psychology of survivors, their guilt, their desire to rescue others. If they could feel some power in their lives, they might avoid the overwhelming helplessness that they couldn't save those they most wished to. "You can never get enough of a substitute," said American philosopher and essayist Eric Hoffer. Yet Pip tries to rescue two very difficult people, and believes he fails.

Pip's attraction to Estella might be understood as evocative of his desire to rescue her, this poor child living with that horror, Miss Havisham. Any person not drawn to save her would have run away from the scene. Instead, Estella's plight draws in Pip.

Even in the contemporary world, not much can be done to overcome the sort of hate indoctrination that Estella receives from Miss Havisham. "Break their hearts my pride and hope, break their hearts and have no mercy," (p. 95) she tells her adopted child. Young people who grow up in such environments typically don't turn out well. They seem to leave bombs in backpacks in crowds. The power of love fails to transform them. There's more psychology to use than Pip had available in the mid-nineteenth century, yet such people brought up like Estella render helpless highly trained specialists. Ask anyone involved in educating the poor or the angry or alienated. Readers ought to feel much kindness towards Pip for making such a bold, full-hearted attempt to rescue Estella.

The same with Magwitch. He tells Pip at one point of his upbringing: abandoned, desperate, in and out of jail, "A terrible hardened one," (p. 346) Magwitch quotes his jailers as saying. Then and now, criminologists don't know how to rescue someone like Magwitch. Science might give someone a new heart, or put 10,000 songs on a telephone, but human knowledge still doesn't extend to the ability to make a Magwitch a happy or decent human being.

A reader might then say to Pip that he was trying to do the impossible with both of them. He revealed his kindness, his capacity for compassion, his desire to help people in great need. He ought not to feel his own personal inadequacy. Human knowledge doesn't yet include an understanding of how to do what he tried. There's no blame to him in trying to help these unfortunate ones.

But at the end of the novel, Pip may feel some sense of release. It might even be speculated that this survivor had to go through his own failure at rescue, so that he might grieve completely. The reader saw Holden Caulfield finally crushed by the grief he had carried for years. There is liberation in that total loss to grief. Pip's sadness might be with him for the rest of his life, but perhaps, like Holden, it may not cripple him, or determine the way he behaves in life. Pip might be looked on with much respect for a life lived with honest, painful self-reflection and love.

If Pip gets viewed this way, readers might be closer to forgiving their own failures, when the time comes.

Chapter 5

How They Did Politics
Way Back in the Day

Reading: *Oedipus the King* by Sophocles, translated by Robert Fagles.

This course takes a theatrical approach to the play. There are other approaches that assert that the contemporary world ought to appreciate the different perspective of the Greek world at the time. They say people do a disservice to the play to view it through modern eyes. But Sophocles and Shakespeare embraced the theater, not the university. Around today, they'd live and write in Hollywood, New York, or London, not Cambridge, Berkeley, or Oxford. As theater, then, it might be viewed as an interaction between creators and an audience. What is relevant would be the effectiveness of this interaction.

Shakespeare's plays are often set in different times, with guns instead of swords in *Romeo and Juliet*. There might be a visual clue in *Hamlet*, like Polonius nodding his head knowingly in Kenneth Brannaugh's film version, when Claudius tells Polonius he intends to send Hamlet "to England." This transforms Polonius from a doddering old fool to one who assents to Hamlet's murder. Current tastes dictate that the Bard's words and plots remain the same, unlike the nineteenth century's sometime staging of Romeo and Juliet waking up at the end, to much joy. While such an ending might be preferred, current tastes dictate that a staging of a play adhere at least to the original words, if sometimes sections get deleted.

It is interesting to consider the dramatic possibilities of these ancient plays, how an audience might connect over the millennia to portrayals of the struggles of such human beings. For students to consider an ancient Greek play ought not to be an anthropological enterprise. The effort becomes seeing Oedipus as a human being.

This play also reveals the powerful interplay between the conscious and the unconscious. Characters contain so many secrets, so much no one says out loud. The drama arises from watching it explode.

The gods the Greeks invoke might best be understood as their version of Santa Claus, Tooth Fairy, Easter Bunny. Students hear Sam Cooke's wonderful song, "Cupid," *Cupid draw back your bow/and let your arrow go/straight to my lover's heart/for me . . . .* Does Cupid exist? If he doesn't, why is someone singing a song to him? "It's a way of talking about some desire the singer has," say my students. Santa and the others might be considered as a way to embody generosity, or rites of passage, or the coming of Spring.

These Greek gods ought to be understood far more in psychological terms than religious ones.

Dionysus, in *The Bacchae,* embodies the power of intoxicants. These Greek gods express the unconscious. Freud's name for a psychological concept, *The Oedipal Complex,* arises from this understanding of the psychological dimension in this play. When the characters in *Oedipus* are talking about *the gods,* they mean aspects of human qualities. Even though the characters may use the word *belief* in talking about the gods, they are best understood as *myths.*

But this view of the play also arises from a position about *belief.* In a moral view, human suffering is an absolute. *Beliefs,* no matter their source, ought to be considered as relative, expressive of a person and his or her stance in the world. *Belief* can be quite powerful as a basis for action. But it cannot be used as a justifier for causing human suffering. Terrorist jihad, or killing of homosexuals, based upon *belief,* can't be moral. The Old Testament's story of Abraham obeying an order from God to kill his own son is not moral. *Belief* can't be moral if it involves inflicting suffering on other human beings.

Killing an infant, because the Oracle at Delphi said so, is not a moral deed.

Oedipus the King becomes a political drama. Oedipus and Creon struggle for state power. Everything they say, to each other and to the chorus, ought to be understood in the current concept of *spin.* They angle for influence, to get the chorus and the audience to see things their way. Scandal gets involved. The Watergate Scandal question, *what did he know and when did he know it,* becomes a powerful tool to understand the characters and their motivations.

Consider the chorus as a character. Maybe they might be considered a collective one, but what they say isn't truth or wisdom or commentary outside the drama itself. They ought to be heard as any character on the stage might be, as expressing their human desires and thoughts. From Shakespeare's soliloquies to the asides of characters in *Modern Family* or *House of Cards,* these characters vie for the audience's understanding and support. They may be speaking confidentially to their off-stage listeners, but they are still in role. These speeches constitute part of the drama, not something separate from it.

To get at the play itself, the backstory needs to be clearly seen. Sophocles' audience would be familiar with the mythological tale of Oedipus, part of their cultural heritage, as would be Santa Claus or Easter Bunny tales in our culture. In an effort to dispel an expectant dad's anxiety, Laius goes to the fortune-teller at Delphi, who tells him his son will kill him and marry his wife/the child's mother.

What Freud goes on to say, and Delphi might have added, is that all dads endure this. Boy children desire to have their first love-object all to themselves. Affection between dads and sons overcomes such murderous passions. Son lets dad have his honey. He'll go find his own. No big deal. It's just human life being lived over time. Except for this dad. He binds the newborn's ankles together, gives orders to mom to destroy the child. She gives it to a shepherd to set the child on a rock to die. The shepherd, rather than waste a perfectly good baby, gives it to his buddy, who then gives it to the childless king and queen of his place, Corinth. Lucky boy.

Perhaps Uncle Creon bribed the Delphi prognosticators to stress the deadly aspects of this particular child to dad. Creon understood dad's son was his chief rival for political power. This follows from the political-investigative notion that whoever benefits most from some action may be the perpetrator of it.

When the grown-up Oedipus hears of this prophecy, he leaves his adoptive parents immediately. Particularly because the chorus and everyone seems to jump all over Oedipus for his Tragic Flaw, his nobility and self-sacrifice in this regard ought to be noted. He doesn't want to cause death and dishonor to his beloved parents. He splits. The young man behaves as a loving son.

Ah, but road rage gets him going. He kills three bodyguards out of four and their boss. It might be asked how it is that a king had such a lousy Secret Service that they couldn't handle one young man. Laius seems to have been quite baffled by the Sphinx. Maybe it ought not to be too surprising that incompetence pervaded his governance. FEMA ought not to be blamed solely for Katrina. Then Oedipus meets the Sphinx. Of course, he could solve the riddle that baffled his dad. What goes on four legs in the morning, two at noon, and three in the evening? Dad couldn't answer since he was so fearful of succession. "Man," says the person entering his prime. And that was that.

Oedipus goes into Thebes. It's then that students are shown three pictures and asked to identify them: my dad in late middle age, sitting in a golf cart, arms crossed over his chest, grinning; my younger son's high school graduation picture; my wedding photo. "Who are these three people?" Over all the years students have seen these photos, they have nailed them, every time. Humans possess great ability to recognize kinship.

Some in the crowd at Thebes, there to welcome the hero who overcame the Sphinx, might have whispered to their friends, "Oh, I guess mom didn't have that baby killed after all." The clever young man might also very quickly figure out which big shot he had killed earlier in the day. But the town, out of gratitude and desire for a good ruler, offers to make him king, rather than inquire what happened to his bumbling predecessor. Thebes isn't a democracy. It was hard to get rid of an idiot king. Oedipus keeps quiet. The townspeople do, too. Creon, realizing he can't politically assault the new hero, bides his time.

Mokita, in the Kiriwina language of New Guinea, means "the truth that everyone knows, but no one speaks about."[1] It's a conspiracy of silence. A whole lot of people knew Lance Armstrong, or Barry Bonds, had to accomplish their athletic feats with chemical help. But it benefitted everyone involved in cycling and baseball to put forth such heroes. *Mokita*.

The mother knew her grown son from the moment he walked into Thebes after making the Sphinx go away. She even suggests the physical similarity in line 818 when she describes Laius as ". . . his build . . . wasn't far from yours." What better way to get revenge on her narcissistic, murderous former husband than fulfilling the very prophecy that got him going in the first place? How best to expiate her guilt for cooperating in the infant's destruction? Wouldn't it be a fine way to dishonor this hated man by having sex with his son? She had no more children with Laius, but four with Oedipus. She embraced the opportunity with the young man.

Oedipus, of course, didn't know Laius was his dad. He believed he had left him far away. All he has to do is remain king, keep his rival Creon at bay, and all will be well.

Then the play starts.

The plague that hit Thebes presents Oedipus with the first crisis he can't solve. Politicians take human problems as their rightful burden. Think of Jenna Marbles' hilarious riff on her online show where she falls up the stairs, shows her dirty sink, complains about the book she's reading, gets her period, again, all with the sarcastic litany of "Thanks, Obama!" Thebes probably suffers from cholera, or another germ-caused disease. Humanity will have a proper diagnosis and cure in a couple thousand years. Yet, Oedipus understands that his political future rides on appearing like he's successfully battling the plague.

He shows great sympathy to his suffering Thebians. Says he'll do all in his power, etc., etc. Sends his political rival Creon back to Delphi for their insight. It may be like Obama asking Fox News for advice, but he's got to show activity. At least, it serves to get his rival out of town. Maybe Creon will fail, or come back with some easy advice. Perhaps Oedipus might be beguiled by Creon's claim, during the play, in lines 654–55, ". . . who in his right mind would rather rule and live in anxiety than sleep in peace?" Especially as Creon behaves at the end of the play, once he's got state power, the audience knows his earlier statements disavowing his desire for the crown constitute the usual spin of the second-in-command. Everybody was so surprised when Pinochet proved to be a ruthless dictator. He had been obsequious to Allende.[2]

Creon makes his move. Tells Thebes it has to avenge the death of the previous king in order to stop the plague. Oedipus says what he has to about the cold case. But language betrays him. Every time Creon asserts it was killer*s*-thieve*s*-murderer*s*, *plural*, Oedipus replies with the *singular*. Creon, telling what the oracle said, "Pay the *killers* back . . . ." (line 123), or what the lone survivor reported, "He said *thieves* attacked them—a whole band, not single-handed . . ." (line 139). Oedipus responds to the survivor's report, "A *thief*, . . ." (line 140). He says later, "Now my curse on the *murderer* . . ." (line 280) [my italics].

All this drama becomes so delicious as it is understood they are pretending, posing, obscuring what they know to be true. Only Oedipus doesn't know his true parentage. Oedipus believes he left his beloved parents in Corinth. Once the blind guy, independent of the town, untouchable by state power, gets hauled in to say what no one else will, the house of cards starts to fall around the failing hero. Tieresias wants no part of it at first. He realizes that all sides are colluding in this dangerous political conflict. Oedipus goads him until he blurts out, "I say you are the murderer you hunt" (line 412). Oedipus does what every politician does in such circumstances. He accuses the messenger of conspiracy against him, with his chief nemesis, Creon. Then Tieresias lets fly with the one thing he didn't know: Laius was his dad.

From this moment, when Oedipus starts to let in the personal nature of the crime, the curse he sought to avoid by his principled flight from Corinth actually fulfilled, his troubles develop far beyond political ones. If it was just murder of the old king, he might have been able to maintain his deft political touch. But he killed his dad. Then might come the understanding that his dad sought to kill him when he was nothing more than an innocent infant. Even more crushing, the woman he loved for many years, who bore him four children, had been complicit in the infanticide. Being as clever as he was, he might even have grasped that she recognized him as her son, and chose to wed him out of revenge on Laius. Bill Clinton might not have been able to survive if he thought that Monica Lewinsky was, in fact, his daughter from some long-ago affair.

The chorus, that is, the people of Thebes, want effective rulers. They feel much loyalty to Oedipus, "Never will I convict my king; never in my heart," they convey to Oedipus (line 572). But they have their priorities.

Creon and Oedipus go at it, each spinning for the chorus, trading accusa-
tions, denouncing each other. Only one can win. The other pays with his
life. Such was pre-democratic politics. Oedipus, rendered ineffective by the
plague, now with burgeoning personal grief, doesn't stand much chance
against his challenger. Jocasta, perhaps realizing the conspiracy is starting
to unravel, tries to calm them down, "Aren't you ashamed, with the land so
sick, to stir up private quarrels?" (lines 711–12). She's known for a while of
their rivalry, referring to it as a *private* quarrel. The chorus even wants them
to unite, "Believe [Creon's oath of truthfulness] it, be sensible, give way, my
king, I beg you!" (lines 725–26).

Jocasta, though, in one last attempt to keep a lid on things, doesn't inter-
cede with her husband about Creon after her initial try. The chorus notices
her silence, and asks, "Why do you hesitate?" (line 752). The audience knows
why. Her language also betrays her. As Oedipus tells her Creon accused him
of killing Laius, she asks, "How does he know? Some secret knowledge or
simple hearsay?" (lines 775–76). Who let the cat out of the bag?

Oedipus keeps pushing to know who his father was, past Jocasta admonishing him, ". . . sweep it from your mind forever" (line 1067) and then "Live,
Oedipus, as if there's no tomorrow!" (lines 1077–78). He drives himself to
know. Jocasta, her denial crushed, her rage, depravity, guilt all there visible,
conscious, ends her life.

Oedipus' putting his eyes out might be thought of as an expression of grief
or remorse. But maybe also as a plea for sympathy, so he won't be killed.
It might even be imagined he faked it, to evoke pity, as Nixon did when he
resigned and seemed to have developed a severe case of phlebitis. Pinochet
did the same, when he was put under house arrest in the UK, and released
back to Chile on compassionate grounds as a sick old man.

The wonderful town's people welcome Creon as the new king, "Here he
is, just when we need him. He'll have a plan, he'll act. Now that he's the sole
defense of the country in your place." (lines 1550–53). Oedipus' play for pity
works. He isn't executed for killing Laius. Creon wisely understands that the
chorus still has some feeling for their fallen hero. Obama put the kibosh on
prosecuting Bush and Company for violating international treaties on torture.
No sense making martyrs. Creon does lord it over Oedipus at the end, as
Oedipus begs to keep his children with him. "Still the king, the master of all
things? No more: here your power ends" (lines 1675–76).

The most revealing speech is the chorus' last comment, saying to look
upon Oedipus as an object lesson. The former hero isn't any more use to
them. All blinded and messed up, his dear wife who had tried to kill him as a
baby has just hanged herself, and he's just let in that he unknowingly killed
his own father, they can point to him, as if it was all his fault.

It wasn't. His parents set the whole thing in motion when they decided to kill an infant. The town kept quiet about the identity of this effective new ruler. So did Jocasta, and Creon. This was a crime of the collective. All of them decided upon a course of action. "Chance rules our lives," says Jocasta, in line 1069. No. For her, for the chorus, for Creon, to claim that is only a way to deflect their complicity. Gods and told-you-so's come in handy that way.

This is a political tale of contemporary times. Lots of code words, oblique references, tons of backstory to make what people say and do make sense. The clever man guiding the fortunes of this country right now might understand.

NOTES

1. Quoted in *Cognition: The Thinking Animal* by Daniel T. Willingham, p. 502.
2. Says Heraldo Munoz, in his *The Dictator's Shadow, Life Under Augusto Pinochet.*

Chapter 6

How to Respond to Evil

Reading: *Strength in What Remains, a Journey of Remembrance and Forgiveness* by Tracy Kidder.

An important focus of this course is the attempt to help students avoid cynicism and despair as they confront human suffering resulting from evil. The old might teach the young how humans might respond with courage and determination against great anguish. Young people need as much help as they can to provide an antidote to those who place bombs in backpacks and then walk away.

Tracy Kidder may be one of the best contemporary storytellers. Certainly, his story of Paul Farmer, in *Mountains Beyond Mountains,* in volume one, offered a compelling portrait of a doctor's struggles to bring Boston medicine to rural Haiti. Kidder serves up a good one here, in *Strength in What Remains,* that might bridge Dr. Farmer and Albert Camus' Dr. Rieux, in *The Plague,* which comes up soon in the course.

The book serves to introduce students to the terrible tragedy of Burundi and Rwanda in the mid-1990s, in which one group of Hutus slaughtered almost a million of their countrymen in a couple of months. As students ponder the nature of morality and literature, they ought to know about this. Kidder's story also makes the US look pretty good. NYC's Manhattan and Columbia University provided acceptance, tolerance, help to the young refugee. That is kidder's subject in this book. America was, indeed, the land of opportunity for this desperate soul.

The course builds towards a moral center, a way of organizing all that is good around humanitarian efforts. It establishes a way to judge the good or bad in the world. The effort is to construct a powerful optical instrument.

Kidder tells the story of Deogratias, a Burundi medical student, who escapes from the killing of Tutsis by Hutus in his country, first by fleeing to Rwanda, before the genocide started there. When Rwanda erupts, a fellow medical student helps him to escape to New York City. He delivers groceries, sleeps for a while in Central Park, and then in a derelict building with other homeless people. Some people he delivers groceries to befriend him, and sponsor his admission to Columbia. When he graduates, he finds his way to Paul Farmer and Partners in Health in Haiti. This reawakens in Deo the desire to found a health clinic in Burundi. By the end of Kidder's tale, Deo has returned to Burundi and the clinic has been established.

Despite all that he's experienced, Deo's dedication to building this health clinic in his country suggests someone with much soulfulness and deep abiding faith in humanity. The book seeks to inoculate students against feeling sorry for themselves, or giving up in despair, no matter what happens to them in life. They will have before them, in their minds, this young person, and his example of rebuilding and doing good, to oppose horror.

> One day a woman approached Deo with her head bowed and said, "You don't know me, but I want to say that I am so sorry for what happened." Deo suspected that she was confessing to some offense against his family during the war. Her words worried him. If people thought he planned revenge, they might try to kill him first. But it seemed to Deo that Kayanza [the site of his medical clinic] was becoming a "neutral ground," a place where Tutsis from the mountains and Hutus from the lakeside could mingle without fear. A place of reconciliation for everyone, including him. And he hoped he wasn't dreaming. "What happened happened," Deo said to the woman. "Let's work on the clinic. Let's put this tragedy behind us, because remembering is not going to benefit anyone." (p. 259)

This book and its message may lie dormant in students' consciousness. They've got many years before they need to make decisions in their lives about careers, how they might be of use in the world. The book establishes an image of what may be possible. Students read the book, talk about it some, then the class goes on to other things. But it lies there latent until such time as it may serve as a beacon.

Chapter 7

American Silence

Reading: Selections from *The Decision to Drop the Atomic Bomb* by Gar Alperowitz.

*** *** ***

You who dropped a nuclear bomb on Japan, even though Japan was ready to negotiate an end to the war. How many acts of oppression, tyranny and injustice have you carried out, O callers to freedom?

from "Letter to America" by Osama Bin Laden, November 24, 2002, *The Guardian Unlimited.*

Thebian citizens and their silence help connect students as the class scrutinizes America's collective silence. Some kinds of insight into the human condition can be gained only by humility. Considering Alperowitz's view of this historical moment allows students to engage with the historical material as an artist might, by getting beyond the myths Americans have told themselves about what happened. This investigation also hopes to demonstrate how the choices that individuals make do determine what happens, not the other way around.

Posing the question about dropping the atomic bomb introduces the moral theme of this course. Was this decision right? Many say, even to this day, that killing those largely civilian populations in Hiroshima and Nagasaki was needed to end the war with Japan in 1945. Is this true, from the view almost seventy years later? Students ponder the relationship of morality and violence.

This inquiry places the events of the mid-twentieth century, namely World War II, directly in the field of study. So much contemporary literature has arisen from that time. To delve into the horror humans perpetrated upon each other in those years will allow art and literature to connect most deeply to students. Osama Bin Laden's view may not seem all that revolting, if Americans embrace how much that war made monsters of all its participants. This Alperowitz selection helps prepare students to read Albert Camus' *The Plague.*

Depending on how it is calculated, the atomic bombs dropped on Hiroshima and Nagasaki took 250,000 to 400,000 lives, with about 150,00 perishing immediately, and many more from radiation sickness and cancers over the ensuing weeks, months, and years. Alperowitz shows that these bombings, at the very end of World War II, had little military effect on the war itself. American officials, from President Truman on down, perpetrated the myth that these bombs were necessary for ending the war, that without them Americans would have lost close to a million soldiers in an invasion of Japan. Most Americans, even today, hold this view.

At the time, U.S. officials knew Japan was terribly beaten. Americans offered unconditional surrender. The Japanese replied, in the spring of 1945, that they wished only to keep their emperor as a unifying symbol of the nation. That was the only point of disagreement. Japanese officials asked for clarification of the surrender terms. American officials promised to get back to them. They didn't. They didn't want the war to end.

America had spent huge amounts of money to build this powerful new weapon. It stood to give America much sway over the Soviet Union in the postwar world. Americans were still very mad at the Japanese for having started the war, despite America's devastating bombing campaign on Japanese cities, which included 100,000 deaths from the firebombing of Tokyo.

America didn't want the Soviets to be involved in the postwar rebuilding of Japan. It wanted the war to end before they invaded. So in late spring and early summer, when America might have said, "Keep your Emperor. Actually, he will be needed, to tell your people to stop fighting," it waited for the atomic test in mid-July. When that showed how much this weapon might do for America in the postwar world, peace with the Japanese wasn't pursued.

Alperowitz quotes U.S. admiral William D. Leahy's statement a few years after the war:

> It is my opinion that the use of this barbarous weapon at Hiroshima and Nagasaki was of no material assistance in our war against Japan. The Japanese were already defeated and ready to surrender.

And Dwight Eisenhower, who had been Supreme Allied Commander of the Allied Expeditionary Force, at the end of his presidency, on being informed of Truman's intention to drop the atomic bombs on Japan, stated

> I voiced [to Secretary of War Stimson] my grave misgivings, first on the basis of my belief that Japan was already defeated and that dropping the bomb was

completely unnecessary, and secondly because I thought that our country should avoid shocking world opinion by the use of a weapon whose employment was, I thought, no longer mandatory as a measure to save American lives.

Alperowitz also cites:

less than a year after the bombings an extensive official study by the US Strategic Bombing Survey published its conclusion that Japan would likely have surrendered in 1945 without atomic bombing, without a Soviet declaration of war, and without an American invasion.

He links to the poet Maya Angelou, in her Inaugural Day, January 20, 1993, poem,

History, despite it wrenching pain,
Cannot be unlived, but if faced
With courage, need not to be lived again.

Alperowitz continues:

Hiroshima and Nagasaki—now—I think, have very little to do with the past.

How we choose to deal with them, I believe, may have everything to do with the future.

Alperowitz shows that a few people, mainly Secretary of State James Byrnes and President Harry Truman, were the ones who made the decision to use the atomic weapons on Japanese population centers. Alperowitz insists that it wasn't mere momentum, or historical forces beyond the control of individual people. These people understood the terrible effects of the bombs, and decided, not for military reasons but under the cover of war, to use the weapons. They might have decided differently.

As the class approaches the study of European history and its literature, nothing much can be gained from a position of moral superiority that regards others as the perpetrators of the terrible things done in that time. Only in blindness can Americans assert that they only fought back. Students must understand that all humanity shares in the horror of that time. The moral issues that arise from the literature the course considers are all of humanity's issues. This is why Americans need to do away with the myth of the war-necessity for the use of the atomic bomb.

Perhaps it is here, most poignantly, that we confront our own reluctance to ask the difficult questions—for even if one were to accept the most inflated estimates of lives saved by the atomic bomb, the fact remains that it was an act of violent destruction aimed deliberately at large concentrations of non-combatants . . .

To poke through these old ashes obviously raises the most troubling kinds of questions about the nature of decision-making in our democracy, the quality of our leaders, even the moral integrity (or superiority?) of our nation . . .

No nation can claim perfect virtue or absolute moral superiority. An honest confrontation with Hiroshima is important for its own sake, and as a way to help us achieve a better understanding of ourselves—one which may be the precondition to a different, better form of global understanding in the new century. Reinhold Niebuhr was right in 1946 to insist that we must "admit the moral ambiguity of all righteous people in history . . ."

To confront Hiroshima requires that if we choose to be silent we know what it means to be silent—to be acquiescent.

This is a huge challenge for young students. But it is, indeed, the task before anyone who reads the literature of the last century. It doesn't matter so much if Alperowitz convinces students about the specific issue. However they decide on the issue for themselves, they will develop some familiarity with the intellectual and moral struggle with the myths that form America's sense of itself.

Chapter 8

What can Be Learned From the Twentieth Century

Readings: "Holocaust: The Ignored Reality" by Timothy Synder[1] and "What Have We Learned, If Anything?" by Tony Judt.[2]

With both of these writers, students are introduced to two outstanding contemporary historians and public intellectuals. Both have researched and written extensively about twentieth-century European history. They offer thinking that challenges Americans' and students' typical understanding of World War II and its terrible events.

Timothy Synder writes to correct the common image of Auschwitz as central to the history of the destruction of European Jewish civilization. He believes this obscures too much of those terrible events. People regard Auschwitz this way, he claims, because a fair number of people survived, and, living in Western Europe or the United States, were able to write about their experiences. He contrasts this to historians writing in Iron Curtain countries where regimes prevented them from writing about the Jewish nature of Nazi depredations. In terms of the magnitude of the killing, Synder argues that people ought to focus much more to the east, where the extermination of Jewish people was mostly complete by 1942.

Synder also wants to shift the focus of Stalin's horrors from the Gulag, as extensive and awful as that prison system was, to the events in the 1930s, in Belarus and Ukraine. In those places, the Soviet intent was not incarceration and slave labor, as it was in the Gulag, but starvation and population removal. His writing expands the true time of depredations to start in 1930, and not ending until Stalin's death in 1953.

He wants people to view Hitler and Stalin as essentially collaborating in the killing of civilian populations, each for his own purposes. They shared

greatly in the horror. Against their ideologies, he posits "the ethical commitment to the individual." This is what art, particularly the literary arts, poetry
and fiction, might do.

Tony Judt offers a history-sermon, an essay about how Americans view
war. He focuses on how Americans regard World War II. In relative terms,
the United States did not share anywhere near as much suffering and death as
did other nations. There were almost no U.S. civilian deaths during the war,
compared to the millions upon millions in most of the other combatants, like
Russia, China, Germany, and Japan, and the many thousands in England and
France. He believes that for this reason America learned the wrong lessons
from the war.

> As a consequence, the United States today is the only advanced democracy
> where public figures glorify and exalt the military, a sentiment familiar in
> Europe before 1945 but quite unknown today . . . . Indeed, the complacent neo-
> conservative claim that war and conflict are things Americans understand—in
> contrast to naive Europeans with their pacifistic fantasies—seems to me exactly
> wrong: it is Europeans (along with Asians and Africans) who understand war
> all too well. Most Americans have been fortunate enough to live in blissful
> ignorance of its true significance.

This carries over to the American understanding of terrorism. All sorts
of violent groups with far different aims get pushed into one large entity,
which America attempts to battle. Hasn't gone so well, Judt claims, because
Americans don't have much feeling for the issues, national, ethnic, religious,
or social or political, that drive people to organize violence. He also sees that
Americans divide the world into the good guys against the bad guys. This
allows the good country to dehumanize and torture the ones labeled bad.

Writing at the end of the first decade of the twenty-first century, Judt
observes this about American wars on terror and Iraq:

> Far from escaping the twentieth century, we need, I think, to go back and look a
> bit more carefully. We need to learn again—or perhaps for the first time—how
> war brutalizes and degrades winners and losers alike and what happens to us
> when, having heedlessly waged war for no good reason, we are encouraged
> to inflate and demonize our enemies in order to justify that war's indefinite
> continuance.

Again, as with Alperowitz's piece, it isn't so much a matter of whether students agree with either Synder's or Judt's point of view. They gain exposure
to some thinking about this time in humanity's history. This will help them
achieve greater insight when they begin to consider literature that arises out
of the consciousness formed from this time.

NOTES

1. From *The New York Review of Books*, May 1, 2008.
2. From *The New York Review of Books*, July 16, 2009.

Chapter 9

A Vigilance That Must Never Falter

Reading: *The Plague* by Albert Camus.

Anyone alive immediately after World War II would have had the same question: What hope is there? With a world recoiling in horror from the deaths some people perpetrated on others, how can anyone claim good in humanity? Camus in his novel sought to address this still urgent topic.

He employs a metaphor, of plague standing for war. This allows him to unite all of humanity on one side. The enemy becomes the nonhuman, rather than separating people into the good (?) and the bad. Everyone fights against death. In the early chapters, Camus conflates plague with pestilence and with war.

> Everybody knows that pestilences have a way of recurring in the world; yet somehow we find it hard to believe in ones that crash down on our heads from a blue sky. There have been as many plagues as wars in history; yet always plagues and wars take people equally by surprise.
>
> How should [the townspeople] have given a thought to anything like plague, which rules out any future, cancels journeys, silences the exchange of views. They fancied themselves free, and no one will ever be free so long as there are pestilences. (pp. 34–35)

Camus creates a narrator, acknowledged at the end of the story, very much involved in contending with the plague as a doctor. Dr. Rieux deals every day with the plague's sick and dying, "A never-ending defeat," (p. 118) he tells his friend Tarrou. But Rieux endures this because

41

there are sick people and they need curing. (p. 117)

It is the work itself that keeps him going, despite the constant deaths. Tarrou asks Rieux, "Who taught you all this, doctor?" Rieux replies, "Suffering" (p. 118). This becomes Rieux's philosophical anchor in the world. He would work against suffering, as a way to ward off despair, or feelings of helplessness.

How are people to understand that some human beings shoot others, just because they are members of a group they despise? Or gas them, chop them up with machetes, drop or place bombs that destroy them? Just this morning in *The New York Times* came a report of the killing of hundreds of Syrian men, women, and children, killed because they belonged to a sect of Islam at variance with the killers' beliefs. The numbers of dead were nowhere near as many as American atomic bombs vaporized, but this evil seems to endure over the decades. Why do humans do this?

Rieux offers his view:

> The evil that is in the world always comes of ignorance, and good intentions may do as much harm as malevolence, if they lack understanding. On the whole, men are more good than bad; that, however isn't the real point. But they are more or less ignorant, and it is this that we call vice or virtue; the most incorrigible vice being that of an ignorance that fancies it knows everything and therefore claims for itself the right to kill. The soul of the murderer is blind; and there can be no true goodness nor true love without the utmost clear-sightedness. (pp. 120–21)

His claim expresses a hopeful and optimistic view. Evil doesn't bind itself inextricably with the human soul. Education can transform it. If it creates enough humility, humans can overcome the arrogance that enables evil. Both educating and humbling themselves are activities human beings can do. If humans understand that "evil always comes out of ignorance," human action has possibilities for contending with evil.

His friend Tarrou adds to this idea with his own challenge, using well the plague-pestilence-war metaphor:

> I know positively . . . that each of us has the plague within him; no one, no one on earth is free from it. And I know, too, that we must keep endless watch on ourselves lest in a careless moment we breathe in somebody's face and fasten the infestation on him. What's natural is the microbe. All the rest—health, integrity, purity (if you like)—is a product of the human will, of a vigilance that must never falter. The good man, the man who infects hardly anyone, is the man who has the fewest lapses of attention. And it needs tremendous willpower, a never-ending tension of the mind, to avoid such lapses. (p. 229)

What is the way to peace, asks Rieux of Tarrou. "The path of sympathy." If it were said that the Japanese sneak attack on Pearl Harbor infected American consciousness, such that Americans in the resulting blindness destroyed Japanese cities, might the way to peace be to feel sympathy both for the blinded Americans, and for their Japanese victims? It might also be pondered if the 9/11 hijackers infected America more recently, given its behavior at Abu Ghraib and Guantanamo.

These are the sort of questions that can arise from Camus' wonderful novel.

Camus leads up to his most difficult challenge with his portrayal of the Catholic priest, Fr. Paneloux, and his two sermons that seek to explain the plague and its suffering in religious terms. He fails miserably, as Rieux comments:

> Until my dying day I shall refuse to love a scheme of things [religious belief] in which children are put to torture. (pp. 196–97)

Offering Camus' assessment of religious belief as trying to find something worthy in human suffering, Fr. Paneloux himself, by the end, doesn't seem to believe it. When he's infected with the plague, he might have been able to be saved, but he refuses medical help. It suggests that in his crisis of faith, he succumbs to despair.

It's on the last page that Camus articulates his own assertion of belief.

> Dr. Rieux resolved to compile this chronicle, so that he should not be one of those who hold their peace but should bear witness in favor of those plague-stricken people; so that some memorial of the injustice and outrage done them might endure; and to state quite simply what we learn in a time of pestilence: there are more things to admire in men than to despise. (p. 278)

But that's not true. Adding up all the atrocities committed in the last 100 years overwhelms whatever there might be to admire in humanity. The horror of the world makes Rieux's claim as demonstrably false as any religious belief. The good doctor might be allowed a moment of exaggerated feeling, there at the end of the plague, with his wife, good friend, and many townspeople gone. But Camus is too much a philosopher, too intent on engaging with the question of what possible good there could be in humanity to take a pass based on mere sentimentality.

Consider that Rieux isn't offering as fact that humanity is admirable. It's his assertion. He can't prove it, but he's been making this claim since the beginning of the story. It is the reality his acts create. By his behavior during the plague, Rieux demonstrated the truth of his belief.

Despite the horror, can readers, nevertheless, claim there's *more to admire*? That's the challenge Camus offers at the end. It's his response to plague-pestilence-war. By living, people can assert what is admirable. Belief in humanity then does not become something static. It isn't merely proclaimed as true, despite all evidence to the contrary in history. How a person behaves actively demonstrates the belief. Camus unites with other believers in trying to live his faith.

Belief "quickens us into verb, pure verb," as Seamus Heaney said.

Chapter 10

Glimpses at the Tragedy That Has Led to a Current Revolution

Readings: "Brokeback Mountain" by Annie Proulx; selections from *Homosexuality and Civilization* by Louis Crompton; and *The Picture of Dorian Gray* by Oscar Wilde.

These three pieces resemble what was done in the volume one course with nonfiction readings about mental illness, and then with a reading of Herman Melville's "Bartleby the Scrivener." Both cases prepare the intellectual ground for a look at a literary work that's often misread. Only now, with a contemporary consciousness, can readers see what dear Oscar hoped they might.

This consideration starts with the contemporary star-crossed lovers' story, "Brokeback Mountain" by Annie Proulx. It's become part of the culture these days, what with the film version making waves. Two young western American working-class men, dressed as cowboys but performing the more ancient role of shepherds, fall in love in the violently homophobic world of the recent past. There's no way they might imagine a life together in such a malevolent culture. Escaping to a tolerant world in San Francisco or Greenwich Village isn't possible for these culturally bound men of limited education, even if they were able to imagine a life free of their self-blame.

They suffer broken marriages, impoverishment, and one is beaten to death by the side of the road. Had they been able to build a life together, based on their love, as a heterosexual couple might do, they might have had a successful ranch. A current view reveals their tragic plight.

Louis Crompton's book documents the enduring legacy of gay people throughout human history. Through their art forms, in poetry, written myths, and sculptures, he shows how culturally bound the treatment of homosexuality truly is. In parts of ancient Greece, such sexual expressions were a matter

45

of course. Their army believed gay people fought harder, knowing they were fighting with their lover present in the battle. He shows that the influence of the three Abrahamic religions, Judaism, Christianity, and Islam, allowed for a persecution of gay people. This rationale wasn't present in other world religions.

Crompton writes:

> It can hardly be argued that these horrors [persecution of gay people] were a necessary stage in the development of civilized societies. In China and Japan the philosophical wisdom of Confucianism and the religious teaching of Buddhism did not foster them . . . . In contrast, to look back on the history of homosexuality in the West is to view a kaleidoscope of horrors . . . . (p. 539)

Millions of them ripped and shucked and scattered, indeed. It is with this view of the terrible oppression suffered for centuries by gay people in the West that students then read about Oscar Wilde's young man, Dorian Gray.

People often present the book as some sort of morality tale, of how a young man's corruption gets displaced onto a painting of him, while his young happy life goes on. What's the *corruption*? What's the *sin* they talk about? The rich snotty young man Dorian does unceremoniously dump his hetero-love interest Sybil, which leads to her suicide. Other than that, readers know of no other crime until the end, when, in a fit of rage, Dorian kills the man who painted the picture.

Being a jerk, particularly a jerk about romance, doesn't rise to the level of *crime*. Neither should Dorian be blamed for Sybil's suicide. A rich guy builds up a poor girl's dreams, only to shatter them. Happens all the time. She weeps, maybe eats too much ice cream or drinks too much champagne, then goes on with her life, older but wiser. Sybil's choice to take her life was her own. Only in an examination of the life of Oscar Wilde can readers now get some inkling of what his characters, mired in late Victorian London, might have meant by *crimes* or *depravity* or *sin.* This might go a long way to explaining Dorian's actions at the end of the novel.

The success of Wilde's play *The Importance of Being Earnest* made him quite a celebrity. It also meant shame for his male lover's father, a big shot politician. Ultimately, to save his inheritance, his lover testified in court against Wilde, who was then sentenced to prison for sodomy. Prison wrecked his health, led to his early death. Gay people now regard him as their martyred saint. *The Picture of Dorian Gray* becomes a depiction of gay London at the time, a place of much secrecy, evasion, code words, danger. The novel shows how people behave when homophobia oppresses them.

Basil Hallward, the man who painted Dorian's picture, is in love with this young handsome man. "He is absolutely necessary to me," (p. 7) he tells their mutual friend Harry. Lord Henry, or Harry, becomes something of Wilde's voice of introduction to and interpretation of this gay world.

To note the curious hard logic of passion, and the emotional coloured life of the intellect—to observe where they met, and where they separated, at what point they were in unison, and at what point they were at discord—there was a delight in that! What matter what the cost was? One could never pay too high a price for any sensation. (p. 42)

It's only now, in contemporary times, that people can say specifically what they were talking about: men loving and having sex with other men.
Harry further observes:

All that [experience] really demonstrated was that our future would be the same as our past, and that the sin we had done once, and with loathing, we would do many times, and with joy. (p. 43)

Harry gives Dorian a book that now can be assumed to be a book about living a gay life.

a psychological study of a certain young Parisian, who spent his life trying to realize in the nineteenth century all the passions and modes of thought that belonged to every century except his own, and to sum up . . . in himself the various moods through which the world spirit had ever passed. (p. 91)

That phrase, "world spirit" becomes the sort of phrase that Crompton might use, in his book. So does the phrase "Greek love" or "New Hedonism" used in the novel. Living in an oppressed world, where great dangers lurk, requires a special language.
Dorian liked the gay life, despite its moments of shame.

That curiosity about life which Lord Henry had first stirred in him, as they sat together in the garden of their friend, seemed to increase with gratification. The more he knew, the more he desired to know. He had mad hungers that grew more ravenous as he fed them. (p. 94)

Dorian seems to understand how Basil's picture of him liberates him:

Eternal youth, infinite passion, pleasures subtle and secret, wild joys, and wilder sins—he was to have all these things. The portrait was to bear the burden of his shame—that was all. (p. 77)

Basil, disappointed or jilted lover, threatens to expose Dorian as gay. That means ruin, prison, maybe death. In this context, Dorian murders the blackmailing Basil. He then blackmails another lover of his, Alan Campbell, to dispose of the body.

Consider how Max, Bigger Thomas's defense lawyer, characterized his murder of Mary Dalton:

> I plead with you to see a mode of *life* in our midst, a mode of life stunted and distorted, but possessing its own laws and claims, an existence of men growing out of the soil prepared by the collective but blind will of a hundred million people. I beg you to recognize human life draped in a form and guise alien to ours, but springing from a soil plowed and sown by all our hands. I ask you to recognize the laws and processes flowing from such a condition, understand them, seek to change them. If we do none of these, then we should not pretend horror or surprise when thwarted life expresses itself in fear and hate and crime. (*Native Son,* by Richard Wright, p. 359)

Bigger Thomas's murders, Max says, become products of *oppression.* If Dorian gets viewed in the same manner, his actions become those of a desperate human being. The novel becomes not so much a tale of the supernatural, or of depravity, but rather of what happens when people find themselves caught in a world that seeks to crush their humanity. Rather than a moral lesson, Dorian's picture becomes that of many people, their frustration, their anger, which twists their lives into tragedy. This reading of literature serves to assist students as they find their way to compassion for such characters.

Chapter 11

Some Remarks about Senior Essays

(See Appendix 1 for list of senior class essay topics)

Essays longer than the (volume one) junior class's 500 words get assigned to seniors, coming in at 750 for the first half dozen, due every week, then up to 1,000 the rest of the year, due every two weeks. But the same format applies: single spaced, word count stated at the top, no names, just i.d. numbers on the back of the last page.[1]

Senior students read a similar combination of literature and nonfiction as the junior class, but the essay topics concentrate more on the ideas emanating from the texts, rather than the juniors' study of the essay form. There's still the mix of personal, historical, political topics, but the literary works more centrally serve as their point of departure.

Most topics[2] urge students to "Think about this . . ." Most of them haven't given much thought just yet to what the topics propose they contemplate and find words for. Some of the topics might be viewed as life-issues, which can be matters of intellectual inquiry, like the concept of *privilege* after reading Seamus Heaney's poems "Oysters" and "From the Republic of Conscience." The same goes for having students articulate their ideas about intoxicating substances after they read *The Bacchae*.

The topic about a personal reflection on a historical moment, EA-4, does serve to connect them with someone in their life, where they have a discussion about history and memory. These prove to be powerful or sweet or touching essays. It's an accessible topic, for them to ask the question of someone, and then report their response. But for all the rest of the topics, what gets put on the page is their initial thinking about the matter at hand, first-time words, often never before expressed.

Comments given back to them seek to deepen, broaden, or challenge their thinking. As with the volume one's junior essays, comments become a way to let writers know someone is reading and taking seriously what they write. It's a conversation in print. What they write down must be considered far more valuable to their thinking and skill development than anything a reader and commentator might offer.

These essay topics get at the large divide between these young people and adults. Teens don't yet think in the theoretical or conceptual terms that the topics call for them to do. To work on closing this intellectual developmental gap becomes a critical endeavor. The topics raise issues, of morality, of the implications of history and historical research, of matters of faith, of their awareness of prejudice, where students don't yet have much understanding. They may have some personal experience, but mostly it's initial thinking.

When they encounter such conceptual thinking later on, their initial forays into these abstractions may start to resonate with them. One former student wrote after her sophomore year in college to tell me that she strongly disagreed with a stance against the death penalty when it was offered in her high school class. When she got to college, and heard Sister Helen Prejean, author of *Dead Man Walking*, an articulate advocate against the death penalty, she said she could then understand what point was trying to be made.

Writing these essays becomes practice for students in going from specifics to theory, or using reason, logic, and evidence to arrive at some conceptual understanding of a topic. The process of writing gives them some experience in evaluating different ways of thinking about a topic. They're not very adept yet at handling competing observations. Is Hamlet a spoiled privileged brat? A madman? A misogynist? An intellectual caught in a vicious world? A man anticipating The Enlightenment? Is alcohol something good or something bad? Was World War II a triumph for us, or did Americans share in the shame of it all? Students lament that the essays for the senior year are harder than the junior-year ones. That's the plan. They become acquainted with how intellectual inquiry leads to further questions, never to a conclusion. There's always more digging, more to say.

Welcome, students, to the world of the mind.

NOTES

1. See my earlier discussions of essays in the (volume one) junior-year sections, Chapters 2, 15, 21, 28, 31 and Appendix 5.

2. See Appendix 1 of this volume for a full listing of senior-year essay topics.

Chapter 12

To Russia, with Love and Poetry

Readings: "First Loves" by Michael Ignatieff; selected poems by
Anna Akhmatova

This essay and the poems give a chance to offer a bit of Russian history in the
first half of the twentieth century, and some smattering of the intellectual cur-
rents of that time. Russian people regard poets far differently than American
people do. Joseph Stalin, the world's most vicious dictator,[1] couldn't touch
the poet Anna Akhmatova, because she was a combination of how Americans
would regard a rock star, an evangelist, and a sports hero.

To consider these people at this time presents a huge challenge for Americans, here in this free, rich, open society. A concerted effort needs to be made
to imagine the fear and deprivation of a police state, or a nation invaded by
a malevolent, implacable foe. It does not suffice to be tourists, gawking at a
strange land and customs. Studying the poetry of another country means becoming anthropologists, connecting what is read with what is most deeply human.

Ignatieff writes mainly of Isaiah Berlin, one of the outstanding political
philosophers of modern times. He was a Russian emigre who became an
academic and public intellectual in Britain. Berlin had two meetings with
Akhmatova on visits as a British diplomatic official after World War II. From
the suffering of the Russian people under Stalin, particularly of Akhmatova,
Berlin embraced the idea of freedom as necessary for human life. He had to
defend against many of his colleagues on both sides of the political spectrum.
Berlin was not an ideologue of either the left or the right. Instead, he called
for moderation, understanding that the goals of liberty, equality, and justice
imply that some people will lose, even if this means that others will gain.
Rather than holding a utopian view, he sees a tragic vision of life, where

societies must choose among competing goals. He values democracy, he says, because it does not make the political process murderous.

At the time, many intellectuals insisted that history marched on, and whether individual humans acted one way or another didn't matter too much. As for Berlin, he pointed to Akhmatova as an example of an individual who did stand up to the forces of tyranny, and succeeded.

Ignatieff offers a brilliant essay, connecting political philosophy and history with a love story. Akhmatova's poems might strike students from the great distance, both geographical and historical, as more anthems than poems. But all of Russia admired her. Stalin understood that he couldn't silence her since she articulated the soul of Russia.

Requiem

No foreign sky protected me,
no stranger's wing shielded my face.
I stand as witness to the common lot,
survivor of that time, that place.

Instead of a Preface

During the frightening years of the Yezhov terror, I
spent seventeen months waiting in prison queues in
Leningrad. One day, somehow, someone 'picked me out.'
On that occasion there was a woman standing behind me,
her lips blue with cold, who, of course, had never in
her life heard my name. Jolted out of the torpor
characteristic of all of us, she said into my ear
(everyone whispered there)—'Could one ever describe
this?' And I answered—'I can.' It was then that
something like a smile slid across what had previously
been just a face.

Dedication

Mountains fall before this grief,
A mighty river stops its flow,
But prison doors stay firmly bolted
Shutting off the convict burrows
And an anguish close to death.
Fresh winds softly blow for someone,
Gentle sunsets warm them through; we don't know this,
We are everywhere the same, listening
To the scrape and turn of hateful keys

And the heavy tread of marching soldiers.
Waking early, as if for early mass,
Walking through the capital run wild, gone to seed,
We'd meet—the dead, lifeless; the sun,
Lower every day; the Neva, mistier:
But hope still sings forever in the distance.
The verdict. Immediately a flood of tears,
Followed by a total isolation,
As if a beating heart is painfully ripped out, or,
Thumped, she lies there brutally laid out,
But she still manages to walk, hesitantly, alone.
Where are you, my unwilling friends,
Captives of my two satanic years?
What miracle do you see in a Siberian blizzard?
What shimmering mirage around the circle of the moon?
I send each one of you my salutation, and farewell.

Courage

We know what trembles on the scales,
and what we must steel ourselves to face.
The bravest hour strikes on our clocks:
may courage not abandon us!
Let bullets kill us—we are not afraid,
nor are we bitter, though our housetops fall.
We will preserve you, Russian speech,
from servitude in foreign chains,
keep you alive, great Russian word,
fit for the songs of our children's children,
pure on their tongues, and free.

—23 February 1942

That last poem, "Courage," has the date attached. It was written during the darkest days of Hitler's invasion, when Leningrad was under siege, and it looked like Russia was going to be conquered and obliterated by the Nazis. Americans have never had that experience. In the last couple of hundred years there's been no event, no moment when the nation felt its civilization, its language, was going to vanish. The Russians, in 1942, felt that way. Akhmatova's poems became a rallying cry for her people faced with this terrible onslaught.

Many contemporary artists have taken the "Instead of a Preface" as their own anthem to assert their ability to describe the horrors they see. That is what artists do. It's the claim, "I can" that gives the inarticulate sufferers much pleasure.

Akhmatova remained in Russia, when many others fled. Her poem "Requiem" might also be thought of as an assertion. She was not going to abandon her people, even if the rulers killed her first husband, imprisoned her son. She would remain. Her poem "Dedication" shows how much she could make good on her "I can."

There may be some cruelty in offering these poems to American students, so comfortable, so safe. They haven't given permission to anyone to treat them this way. They are being shown vast human suffering and large thoughts about democracy and dictatorship. Their protest against such considerations isn't ever overt, most often not even articulated. In their subdued sadness as they leave such classes, they express an awareness of something having been taken from them by the experience they've just had.

In such moments education can feel like subtraction rather than addition.

NOTE

1. A crowded field, with claimants from both Germany and China. Spain, Chile, even Cambodia might assert that theirs did far more with less opportunity. Nevertheless, Uncle Joe, by force of personality, must be given pride of place.

Chapter 13

The Role of the Artist with Culture

Readings: Review of and selections from *Radical Hope, Ethics in the Face of Cultural Devastation* by Jonathan Lear

This essay calls for some thinking in philosophical terms that students have to stretch to get to, but it's such a good essay, and even if students only connect a bit to its linking of imagination and psyche and courage and the struggle against despair and the relation of all that to the making of art, then it's worth every ounce of their energy and time.

Lear writes:

> imagine that all the pieces of a chess game had inner lives. And imagine that each took itself to be a center of agency. I am a knight! I see myself in tribal terms: I am a black knight! I am proud to be a black knight! I think strategically in terms of my possible moves . . . . I understand all the other members of my tribe in terms of the roles they play: and I understand that we are all aspiring to excellence in the sense that we are trying to win. Unbeknownst to me, my world exists because it is protected by a group of humans. These are the guardians of the chess world, who insist that the only acceptable moves are moves that are allowable within the game of chess. From my point of view as a thoughtful knight, the humans are as unknowable as the transcendent gods. But suppose . . . humans got bored with playing this game, and the game of chess goes out of existence. My problem is not simply that my way of life has come to an end. I no longer have the concepts with which to understand myself or the world . . . . The concepts with which I would otherwise have understood myself—indeed, the concepts with which I would otherwise have shaped my identity—have gone out of existence. (pp. 48–49)

It's also difficult because Lear asks students to think of culture as not something absolutely connected to existence, but rather as distinct from it, depending upon the circumstances and possibilities of living. As opposed to Akhmatova's "great Russian speech," Lear suggests, in his study of the response of a Native American tribe, the Crow, that it might be possible for a group of people to reinvent themselves, their language and culture, even what they hold to be of value in living.

Lear talks of Plenty Coups, the leader of the Crow, from the late nineteenth century to well into the twentieth century. Unlike his contemporary Sitting Bull, he chose to capitulate to the whites, transforming his people from hunter/gatherers into farmers. Their entire culture was founded on the idea of a warrior people. Preparing for battle and courage in battle formed the basis of what they valued, how they understood the meaning of their lives. Plenty Coups led his people to give all this up to survive and to try something new.

Considering Plenty Coops's leadership, so opposite that of the battle-to-the-death attitude of Sitting Bull, suggests that students re-imagine the role of the warrior and hero that so imbues Western culture and its literature. It allows students to discuss the notion of moral psychology. Lear offers this as an idea of striving to live in the world with other human beings.

Plenty Coups leads his people into this new life by relating two dreams he had as a boy. This might be understood as the role of imagination in leadership. He relates these dreams, products of his unconscious, as an artist might, to have his people envision a different reality for themselves. This provides an antidote to the despair a conquered people feel as they understand that the military or technological dominance of the conqueror means their culture has no hope of survival. Plenty Coups's vision suggests possibilities beyond their specific culture.

Lear reflects about Plenty Coups's use of the dream as a creative act:

> There is the possibility that our wishes could be integrated into an overall functioning of our imaginative capacity in such a way as to facilitate a creative and appropriate response to the world's challenges. We thus have room for the idea of imaginative excellence when it comes to ethical life. This is the claim that needs to be defended on Plenty Coups's behalf: that his dream may have expressed his wishes—both for himself and for the tribe—but that it also responded to the anxiety that his tribe shared. This anxiety was itself a realistic response to the world. And the radical hope that young Plenty Coups's dream generated was itself a manifestation of imaginative excellence. It enabled the tribe to face its future courageously—and imaginatively—at a time when the traditional understanding of courage was becoming unlivable. (p. 117)

All this may be quite different from heroic notions imbued in American culture. Lear pushes students to think in philosophical and radically speculative terms. Consider, for example, our huge cultural resistance to a world without automobiles, individual gun ownership, meat, or even American football. Each of these cultural artifacts might be viewed as damaging human welfare. Yet, the country defends these things as necessary elements of American life. To imagine the world without them would be the province of artists, creating psychic space in the collective imagination, as Plenty Coups did, with his dreams.

> That Plenty Coups could formulate such an ideal and pass it along—at a time when traditional ideals were losing their vibrancy—is, I think, his greatest achievement. (p. 141)

Art then may liberate people from a culture rather than supporting it or explaining the culture. Artists become those who show new ways to imagine living that haven't yet been conceived. Only one class gets spent on Lear's ideas, but they pervade the entire enterprise of the course.

> Plenty Coups's dream—and his fidelity to it—also enable him to live what Aristotle would call a complete life. In spite of the devastation to traditional Crow life, Plenty Coups's dream became a thread through which he could lead his people through radical discontinuity. In sticking to his dream, he unified his life across this discontinuity: and at the end of his biological life, he was able to see his life as having a unity and a purpose that was confirmed by the unfolding of events. (p. 148)

Chapter 14

Afterwards, How Do You Live a Life?

Reading: *Beloved* by Toni Morrison.

With Morrison's skill, readers end up understanding why a mother might kill her children. They even grow to care about Sethe, this poor, tortured, traumatized mother. Morrison evokes such vivid characters, Sethe, Paul D, and Baby Suggs. Students won't be the same people when they finish reading the novel. Some of art might be termed the history of tears.

Although the course focuses on literature from Europe, this is a work by a contemporary African-American woman. It's in the senior class, partly because students are a year older and perhaps more willing to allow themselves the experience of the novel. It also has elements of ancient Greek and Russian literary traditions. Morrison found her inspiration for the novel in a nineteenth-century newspaper account of a "Modern Medea." Like Richard Wright in his *Native Son*, these African-American writers relate to human suffering and oppression in ways that evoke Dostoevsky. The novel serves to offer a sense of the underlying unity of art, across boundaries and nationalistic claims. A bit of a mash-up with the offering of an American author this year offers opportunity rather than inconsistency.

This novel's readers witness what oppression does to the human psyche. Sethe is driven out of her mind by rape, by torture, and, particularly, she remarks many times, by having her "milk stolen," sucked by her white captors to amuse themselves and humiliate her and her husband for running away. She finally does escape across the same Ohio River that Eliza ran across with her child in *Uncle Tom's Cabin*. She resolves that she and her loved ones would never return to the horror of slave life. Threatened with capture, she makes good on her vow with one of her children, by killing that

child with a saw. The man who had helped her escape over the river stops her
from killing her infant.

This is the prologue. The real action of the novel comes after her child's
murder and her time in jail. Her infant born on the flight to freedom is now a
teen. How does anyone live a life after this? How can a human being recover?

Enter Beloved.

Students ought not to think of Beloved as a character, in the typical sense
of an imagined human being, who incorporates individuality, personality, and
an awareness of existing in time. Beloved's not just one ghost, but rather,
as Morrison makes clear in later chapters, a collective one. She represents
not only the death of Sethe's *crawling already* child, but all the deaths of
kidnapped Africans from the slave trade. As Morrison says on the dedication
page, Sixty Million and more. As ghosts might be seen as the products of the
unconscious, Beloved embodies Sethe's rage, guilt, and longing to have her
murdered child return.

"Anything dead coming back to life hurts," (p. 35) observes the young
white woman, Amy Denver, who helps Sethe deliver her child as she's fleeing slavery. As Beloved becomes the agent through which Sethe recovers her
full humanity, this ghost will make this mother suffer. First would come the
pleasure, of her grown child's return, cheating death itself. Then the ghost's
rage, as it realizes it's not alive, and the murderer believes all is well. Beloved
tries to choke her, gets thwarted. Then she enraptures Sethe in a narcotic-like
haze, and drives away Sethe's lover Paul D. The trance is broken only at the
end of the novel, by the intervention of the community. Then Sethe at long
last can begin to grieve, "She was my best thing," Sethe laments, as Beloved
flees. Sethe might then have the possibility of a life with Paul D, as the novel
ends.

Morrison suggests that only going through all the feelings of the past can
a person live in the present. All the longing, all the rage, all the helplessness,
must be encountered, experienced, endured.

Was Sethe wrong, to murder her child? Trauma produced her action at the
moment. But many years later she has this conversation with Paul D, right
after he discovers for himself that she'd killed her child when the slave catchers threatened.

> "Did it work?" he asked.
> "It worked," she said.
> ". . . How did it work?"
> "They ain't at Sweet Home. Schoolteacher ain't got 'em."
> "Maybe there's worse."
> "It ain't my job to know what's worse. It's my job to know what is and to keep
> them away from what I know is terrible. I did that." (pp. 164–65)

Sethe is justifying her actions after many years of reflection. There certainly were psychological reasons for her to do so, to ward off her regret and make the irrational make sense to her. But is this an action that can be justified on moral grounds, that is, outside of a response to trauma? The people around Sethe did not believe it was. Paul D ends that conversation by stating, "You got two feet, Sethe, not four." He claims she denied her humanity in murdering her child. The townspeople, all escaped or emancipated former slaves, shunned her completely. They all had made a decision to endure and persevere, not to destroy themselves or their children, no matter what fate awaited them. Even schoolteacher, a vicious slave owner with no common human feelings toward these people he held in bondage, realized she had transformed herself, was no longer someone within his understanding of human beings, when he arrived to recapture her.

> Right off it was clear, to schoolteacher especially, that there was nothing there to claim. (p. 149)

Even Beloved herself, in trying to choke Sethe, expresses her rage at this mother's action. Should readers defend Sethe's murdering her child, beyond an understanding of how she wasn't in her right mind at the time?

While many students initially view Sethe's action as courageous and morally appropriate, the task becomes to lead them to consider the complications. The African-American students in the classroom descend from those who struggled to survive no matter what the oppression. Their ancestors didn't do what Sethe did. Many other students in the room, of Irish, or Jewish, or Latino heritage, among others, also come from people who kept on. Fault need not be found with Sethe, to say that all these ancients demonstrated courage, nobility, morality, in living and passing on life despite their suffering.

Many years later, a former student spoke of how meaningful this observation was to her. She had been thinking only of how pure Sethe's renunciation of oppression was, how attractive it might be to follow her reasoning. To suggest that courage might reside in struggling to live came as a new thought. It countered her own thinking about suicide. There this student was, sitting over coffee, talking of a reflection out of her present abundant life. Educator's joy.

The novel isn't only about Sethe and her recovery. It's also about Paul D, and Baby Suggs. Morrison presents both these characters as coping with the damage slavery inflicted on them. Paul D had a horse-bit put in his mouth as punishment by the slave master schoolteacher. He reports it made him feel less substantial than the rooster named Mister that Paul D had helped get out of its shell when it was hatched.

> Mister was allowed to be and stay what he was. But I wasn't allowed to be and stay what I was. Even if you cooked him you'd be cooking a rooster named

Mister. But wasn't no way I'd ever be Paul D again, living or dead. Schoolteacher changed me. I was something else and that something was less than a
chicken sitting in the sun on a tub. (p. 72)

Paul D's sense of love contrasts painfully with Sethe's,

For a used-to-be slave woman to love anything that much was dangerous, especially if it was her children she had settled on to love. The best thing, he knew,
was to love just a little bit; everything, just a little bit, so when they broke its
back, or shoved it in a croaker sack, well, maybe you'd have a little love left
over for the next one. (p. 45)

But he understood that Sethe's kind of love represented a different way of
living:

He knew exactly what she meant: to get to a place where you could love
anything you chose—not to need permission for desire—well now, that was
freedom. (p. 162)

Yet, it is his affection for Sethe that does draw her out, have her imagine
another life, after Beloved leaves. These two older people, having endured a
lifetime of suffering, might be able to build a life together. His courage, his
desire, his vision, allow for such a possibility. Paul D emerges as a portrait of
all that might be hopeful in humanity after trauma.

Baby Suggs, on the other hand, connects to despair. Her son worked
innumerable evenings and weekends to buy her freedom. Her body was old
and broken by the time he did. But she became a preacher for the freed and
escaped slave community in Cincinnati.

"Here," she said, "in this here place, we flesh; flesh that weeps, laughs; flesh
that dances on bare feet in grass. Love it. Love it hard. Yonder they do not love
your flesh. They despise it. They don't love your eyes; they'd just as soon pick
em out. No more do they love the skin on your back. Yonder they flay it. And
O my people they do not love your hands. Those they only use, tie, bind, chop
off and leave empty. Love your hands! Love them Raise them up and kiss them
Touch others with them, pat them together, stroke them on your face 'cause they
don't love that either. You got to love it, you! . . . . (p. 88)

But she has such a wonderful celebration when Sethe and her children
show up that it makes the freed slave community jealous. They don't warn
her of the slave catchers coming. Their scorn of her, then their shunning when
Sethe killed her child, ended up crushing her.

So Baby Suggs, holy, having devoted her freed life to harmony, was buried amid a regular dance of pride, fear, condemnation and spite. (p. 171)

Morrison is interested in showing this world, not in making the reader feel good. But why bother telling of this suffering, since slavery doesn't exist anymore? America fought a war over it, the good guys won, and the thing's gone. Why remind a late-twentieth-century audience about people from over 100 years ago?

The ghost, Beloved, abides. The chapter that begins "I am Beloved and she is mine," (p. 210) articulates this collective sense of anguish, rage, desires for revenge. Morrison suggests in her novel a way to understand why white people and African-Americans don't get along very well. There are all these ghosts that impede the ability of people to have truly human relations with each other. America as a country or society has only begun to contend with these ghosts. As Baby Suggs was dying, silently,

until the afternoon of the last day of her life when she got out of bed, skipped slowly to the door of the keeping room and announced to Sethe and Denver the lesson she had learned from her sixty years a slave and ten years free: that there was no bad luck in the world but white people. "They don't know when to stop," she said, and returned to her bed, pulled up the quilt and left them to hold that thought forever. (p. 104)

Morrison in this novel crafts a tale of modern times, its concerns about psyche, recovery, the triumphs and limitations of love, so that the burden of the American Crime in the present day be more deeply understood. If Sethe, Paul D, Baby Suggs can be seen clearly, perhaps human beings today may be able to relate to each other with more kindness and insight.

Chapter 15

Do We Dare?

Reading: *The Tragedy of Hamlet, Prince of Denmark* by William Shakespeare

INITIAL DIFFICULTIES

Much comedy that merges into mockery and trite cultural references block receptivity to this actual play. Everything from Mark Twain's riff in *Huck Finn*, to "Brush Up Your Shakespeare" in *Kiss Me Kate*, to the villain in the movie *The Imposters* being an actor who plays Hamlet, to Tom Stoppard's *Fifteen Minute Hamlet*, makes the audience laugh, and put the drama out of reach.

Perhaps teachers should give up? The play could be retired for a hundred years or so, until the cultural familiarity disappears and the jokes aren't funny. Someone might then rediscover it, like Alice Walker did with Zora Neale Hurston's *Their Eyes Were Watching God*. Wouldn't it be amazing to wander through some museum's storage warehouse, and come upon a painting no one had seen in centuries, titled *Mona Lisa*? Or be traveling in India, and there's this building, the Taj Mahal, that no one had ever seen in pictures? Or to time-travel, back to the first performance of Beethoven's Fifth Symphony?

Given the vagaries of perception or culture, audiences might, nevertheless, miss the greatness. Certainly a *Baltimore Sun* reporter wrote to his editor, after hearing Lincoln's remarks at Gettysburg, "They made no particular impression at the time." But still, there's much power in the freshness, the amazing sense of discovery, that prompt envy for those who first beheld these great works of art. They had the opportunity to simply sit there and have all new worlds and possibilities open up for them.

Even if students might approach the play with clear new eyes, can they weep for Hamlet? He's so contradictory, complicated, confused. Despite moments of tenderness with Ophelia or Horatio or Yorick's skull, he's not all that kind or even likeable. How can young people have any fellow feeling for this self-absorbed child of privilege? If they don't care about him, it really isn't a *tragedy,* despite its name.

Can this tale of Hamlet evoke gut-wrenching sadness despite both the cultural baggage and his portrayal? Why not let flights of angels take him and his story to its rest, and teachers and students do something else with their time?

Akhmatova says "I can." A teacher of literary art takes on a challenge to include this famous but well-worn work in the course. Perhaps a lens can be developed to rescue the play from its familiarity. Much wonderful scholarship has been done on the play. The exploration here doesn't aim to compete with any of that. The intent has been to allow young people to think about the play and Hamlet's plight. By the end of the discussion over the years, Hamlet seems to have meant something to them.

Talking about this play occupies more class time than any other work all year. That's mainly due to the desire, like with *Huck Finn* for juniors in volume one, to engage in more depth with at least one piece of art during the course. Students might then comprehend why this play occupies such a prominent place in the culture. Hamlet's plight emerges as humanity's. If students can weep for him, they might be better equipped to feel compassion for their own struggles.

SOME GENERAL PERSPECTIVES

The play has an audience behold a gangster world. Laws or rules don't govern the contest for power. Like the world portrayed in innumerable movies from *The Godfather* to *No Country for Old Men*, no boundaries or forces exist to contain the struggle for allegiance of armed men and for control of economic resources. Threat comes from everywhere, even your brother. This characterizes the politics of that time and place. To paraphrase Isaiah Berlin, what humanity has achieved with democracy since *Hamlet* (or Elizabethan England) makes such striving for power less murderous.

Everyone in the play lies and maneuvers for advantage. There's much calculation in what they say to each other. Even the soliloquies of Hamlet and Claudius only reveal what they are thinking at the moment, not some truth about themselves. These supposed private utterances even suggest some complicity on the part of the audience. It hears them. It has thoughts and feelings about what the characters convey. The act of listening to soliloquies transforms the audience into participants, perhaps accomplices in their very silence in the conspiracies swirling about Elsinore.

The two women, Gertrude and Ophelia, speak and behave as if they are quite aware they inhabit a man's world. When the women talk in submissive terms, the audience ought to hear them the way an African slave in the American South might say the same thing. When someone has no power in a relationship, offering an independent view can be quite dangerous, and thus to be avoided at all costs. Oppression makes these women cautious. Hamlet might feel scorn for his mama marrying Uncle Claudius so fast, but what's a poor girl to do? Her well-being flows from the man's power and protection. These women ought not to be assessed by contemporary standards. The audience only sees their masks.

Contemporary psychologists now assert that depression and mental illness exist as genuine human illnesses of the psyche. Further, they find that such maladies crippled human beings throughout history. Shakespeare's audience was quite familiar with delusions, hallucinations, altered states of consciousness that might determine behavior. Then and now, those afflicted would try all sorts of coping mechanisms, including "I'm just playing" to help them get by. That's why it will be important to be skeptical of what Hamlet tells the audience about himself. He's afflicted.

Dramatic tragedy arises out of the tension between the choices the characters make and what the audience understands might be possible for the characters to do. Characters might avoid destroying themselves if only they knew something that their behavior clearly indicates they didn't. Sethe claims she had to kill her child, she had no choice. Readers know the life force to be more powerful. Her children wanted to live. Since the Civil War ended slavery soon after Beloved's murder, the audience is quite aware of other possibilities. Romeo and Juliet don't have to slaughter themselves. Somewhere there's a place for them. Annie Proulx's gay cowboys might have been quite happy in Greenwich Village. The anguish of tragedy derives from knowing doom isn't inevitable. Bound either by their own perceptions of themselves, or by their culture and its values, tragic characters lack the ability to conceive of alternatives.

Hamlet ought to be read as firmly grounded in the historical moment of its pre-Enlightenment world. There was no sense of individuality about choosing the path of one's life. People fulfilled their roles, their destiny, doing whatever mama or daddy or God or the king directed them to do. Notions of freedom, or self-fulfillment, or living an independent life, that form much of the contemporary sense of identity, weren't ways that even someone as reflective as Hamlet might have been able to use as he was confronted with his plight.

Bilingual students have an easier time with Shakespeare and his language than English-only speakers, since they've had much experience trying to figure out meaning from context, or getting the gist of what the speaker is saying, even if a word or two doesn't connect. They've developed much more tolerance with the half-knowing or puzzling-it-out aspect of contending with strange language. Certainly Shakespeare needs to be read with footnotes galore, to get to the meaning. Students need to have patience, particularly if they're unfamiliar with this typical second-language task.

Students travel through the entire text of the play, as written, rather than some abbreviation of it, as often happens with film or stage versions. Some scenes or lines often omitted are noted, particularly if these changes alter the meaning of the play.

ACT 1

The opening line of the play, "Who's there?" shouted in fear and threat in a theater performance, can infuse the audience with the sense of the place and time presenting imminent danger. Guards are watching for invaders who might attack at any moment. Their foundries make war materiel round the clock. When the ghost appears and freaks them out, they don't go up the chain of command, to notify the king or one of his minions. They get Horatio, friend of Hamlet. Once he sees the apparition, he too doesn't mention notifying those in command. He wants to tell his friend.

Thus, from the beginning of the play, as in Thebes, characters act in ways that suggest they know more than they let on about their leader. Claudius can't be trusted. Common folk don't comment on how he got to the throne, or to the old king's wife. But when they have to concern themselves with something weird going on, they go to Hamlet, not the man in charge.

The second scene stands in sharp contrast with that war-footing opening scene. All the royals make their grand entrance. Claudius almost casually dispatches emissaries to apply pressure on the old uncle of the threatened invader Fortinbras, so that he will dissuade this young hot-blooded son of the vanquished father from invading. No war speech, no sense of existential threat, seems to disturb Claudius' cat-who-ate-the-canary good feeling. No wonder the castle guards don't trust him.

Why does Laertes have to ask permission of Claudius to leave? There's no sense, from Polonius or Claudius, that he's an essential part of their military defenses, a leader of their armed forces, say. He wants to return to college. You have to ask the king's permission? Sounds like some closed society, like North Korea, or the Sinaloa Cartel. When Claudius tells Hamlet he can't leave, he gives no reason. In true gangster fashion, Claudius seeks to keep his friends close, his enemies closer. The king spends a lot more time, in this scene and throughout the play, worrying about Hamlet and his intentions, than about the threat from Fortinbras, who commands an actual army.

The first thing Hamlet lets the audience know about himself, when he's able to talk directly to them, is basically, *I feel like killing myself.* This utterance suggests anguish, even despair, much deeper than grief at his father's death, or his mother's remarriage. He expresses his anger at his mother in misogynistic terms. He tells the audience of his contempt for his uncle. But it doesn't seem to make sense that he wants to kill himself. Hamlet might be viewed initially through the lens Gertrude and Claudius use to view him, that Hamlet's *holding onto his grief about his father's death. Time to move on, son.* But the guards', and Horatio's, behavior suggest some support for Hamlet's sense that there's something profoundly disturbing about this head couple. When Hamlet, at the end of his first soliloquy says "It is not, nor it cannot, come to good," the audience senses not only Hamlet's struggle with his own personal demons, but his fears for his country.

At the end of the scene, after Horatio has told him about seeing a spirit that resembles his father, Hamlet remarks to the audience, "All is not well. I doubt [suspect] some foul play." The official version of his father's death seems suspicious. All this may not yet be conscious, yet all of them feel it. Claudius, too, would have to sense he's not all that secure in his power. Lots of poses being struck.

Sometimes directors omit the interplay between Laertes and Ophelia in scene 3. That's too bad, since it does show Ophelia having some wit and starch with her brother. As he's offering patronizing advice, she comes right back at him, admonishing him not to tell her to do one thing, and yet himself practice another.

But, good my brother,
Do not, as some ungracious pastors do,
Show me the steep and thorny way to Heaven
Whilst, liked a puffed and reckless libertine,
Himself the primrose path of dalliance treads
And recks not his own rede. (Act 1, scene 3, lines 46–50)

She may hide from those in power over her, but with her brother, she gives as good as she gets.

Students resist a labeling of Polonius' advice to Laertes as Hallmark greeting card-worthy. They want to treasure his words of wisdom.

Neither a borrower nor a lender be,
For loan oft loses both itself and friend
And borrowing dulls the edge of husbandry. (Act 1, scene 3, lines 75–77)

These pearls are attributed to *Shakespeare*. Nooooo. Shakespeare doesn't speak in this play. Characters do. This particular one, an advisor at the court, reflects a person cautious in his bones. He offers advice for those operating in a world where brothers kill each other for political power. To his son going off to college, Polonius' words reveal more about dad's character, than words-to-live-by. One director had Polonius offering these lines, with Laertes and Ophelia behind him, mouthing the words, indicating they had heard these pronouncements many times.

Same with his summary:

This above all: to thine own self be true,
And it must follow, as the night the day,
Thou canst not then be false to any man. (Act 1, scene 3, lines 78–80)

This is nonsense. Polonius implies that the process of *being true to thine own self* was clear and straightforward, rather than a perpetual agony of choosing from among many selves. The entire play involves which *self* Hamlet ought to be true to. Polonius, throughout the play, shows himself quite adept at *being false*. He lies, deceives, and spies in the service of his boss, a murderer of a family member. Nothing about the character suggests a concern with living a life of integrity.

He even undermines his own advice, a few lines later, when he tells Ophelia,

You do not understand yourself so clearly
As it behooves my daughter and your honor. (Act 1, scene 3, lines 96–97)

I'll tell you what your self is, he's saying. This command to his daughter strikes a note that is a tad different than his previous advice.

Much sentimentality surrounds this play that needs poking through.

Putting some focus on Polonius reveals how even this seemingly foolish but innocuous character tries to deceive. If Hamlet displays less craziness than he might seem to show, perhaps Polonius could be viewed as not really all that foolishly benign. Examining Polonius closely serves as a good introduction to this treacherous and deceptive world.

When Ophelia responds, "I do not know, my lord, what I should think," it ought to be understood as responding appropriately in this oppressive world. Hiding behooves everyone in Elsinore Castle.

In scene 4, Hamlet reflects on Claudius' corruption, as the king is getting drunk, while his country faces an imminent invasion. Hamlet also shows some distance from this world he's in. He's able to observe that a bit of corruption ruins the whole man, even if the rest of him is virtuous. Hamlet's thoughtful observations, despite his being so afflicted, so immersed in this dangerous world, become part of what make him so interesting.

In this same scene, after Hamlet goes off to talk with the ghost, one of the guards reflects, "Something is rotten in the state of Denmark." Common folks anywhere, ancient Greece or medieval Denmark, don't really need a ghost to appear, or a blind Tiresias to tell them. They know. When Hamlet hears the Ghost's tale of murder, he responds, "Oh, my prophetic soul! My uncle!" Everyone has a sense, in this world of gangsters, that no one dies a sudden yet natural death. There are no accidents here.

Scene 5 offers the only occasion where the Ghost speaks to other characters besides Hamlet. If a director eliminates this little bit of dialogue, what the Ghost says can then be portrayed as only a product of Hamlet's diseased psyche. The Ghost insists that the guards and Horatio swear themselves to secrecy about the encounter with Hamlet. They don't know what the Ghost said to Hamlet. Why does it care about secrecy for merely appearing to them? Wouldn't spreading the word far and wide, that they've seen the ghost of the departed King Hamlet, and that the Ghost has talked with his son, empower Hamlet in his quest for revenge? Wouldn't such information undermine Claudius' legitimacy?

Perhaps if this were a democratic world, a whispering campaign would erode a leader's standing. But they inhabit a world of gangsters. They don't want their enemies to know what they are thinking, as Vito Corleone might have said.

The last words of the scene reveal something curious that Hamlet tells Horatio and the guards.

Oh cursed spite,
That ever I was born to set it right! (Act 1, scene 5, lines 189–90)

In a play where both Fortinbras and Laertes respond to the killing of their father with intentions of deliberate violence, only Hamlet complains about the bother of it all. The others accept it as what they've got to do. The quest for revenge gives meaning and purpose to their lives. Hamlet's whine, *why me?* suggests his ambivalence. He'd rather be in Wittenberg, reading a book, thinking. He understands that doing what daddy, or at least the Ghost, wants him to do sets him on an exclusive career path. No one leaves The Life alive.

ACT 2

The first part of scene 1, where Polonius instructs a henchman how to spy on his son, often gets cut by directors. This is more understandable than some cuts, given that it chiefly serves only to expand the appreciation for how creepy Polonius truly is. But it so deliciously darkens the sense of Polonius. No prattling fool this, but rather a father willing to use his trade-craft to keep tabs on his son. The audience doesn't have much of a sense why he would bother about keeping such a close eye on Laertes, although at the end of the play, Laertes, full of fury, wants revenge for the death of his father. Claudius views this as a threat to his power, which he deflects toward Hamlet. So maybe even the son of the advisor gets the due diligence of surveillance. In this world, it's best always to watch everyone. Edward Snowden would know.

Scene 2 shows a parallel to scene 1's recruitment of someone to spy on Laertes. But here, it's Claudius and Gertrude wanting to know Hamlet's mind. They act out of concern for the threat Hamlet poses, even though they don't know Hamlet has talked to the Ghost.

Then, in come the emissaries from Fortinbras' uncle. Good news. Fortinbras got told to stop it. He obeys. Then the old uncle gives his nephew money to go fight someone else. What? In this world of gangsters, the threat goes away with a promise? Oh, one more thing: can Fortinbras have permission to walk his full army across your land? Claudius says it's all cool.

No wonder no one goes to Claudius with problems. He's incompetent. He's supposed to ensure the safety of his state. Yet, he allows someone who the day before was going to invade to come on in. Compared to the way he is with Hamlet, so careful and suspicious, Claudius' behavior seems strikingly odd. He's watching closely one person, who wanted to go back to college and was denied permission. Yet, he's placated by flimsy promises from someone with an army whose father was killed by the current king's brother?

Claudius' behavior only makes some sense if he suspects Hamlet knows somehow that he killed his daddy. He projects his guilt onto Hamlet. But the threat from Fortinbras looms through the whole play.

Then Hamlet seemingly has some fun with Polonius. But the scene becomes even more charged if both Hamlet and Polonius are pretending. Hamlet knows what Polonius wants: an answer to the question, *are you upset because Ophelia broke your heart, or because you found out Claudius killed your father?* This is a deadly game. If Polonius finds out what the slain king's son knows, Hamlet's dead. So Hamlet gets goofy. But he's so troubled, he expresses clearly his despair, when Polonius says "I will most humbly take my leave of you" (Act 2, scene 2, line 217).

You cannot, sir, take from me anything that I will more willingly
part withal—except my life, except my life, except my life.

Sometimes directors have these lines delivered as an aside, a brief soliloquy, to increase their sense of true expression. Hamlet indeed lives in a terrible world. That's both truth, and an expression of his affliction. He gets angry, sort of, by the end of the play. But mostly what the audience sees, in contrast to Fortinbras or Laertes' energy and resolve to enact revenge, is Hamlet's crippling depression.

Hamlet offers his most eloquent expression of this despair when he's extracted from Rosencrantz and Guildenstern their confession "My lord, we were sent for," by Claudius, to spy on him:

I have of late—but wherefore I know not—lost all my mirth, forgone all custom of exercises, and indeed it goes so heavily with my disposition that this goodly frame the earth seems to me a sterile promontory . . . . (Act 2, scene 2, lines 307–10)

But Hamlet's not telling the complete truth. He knows partly why he's in such misery. His uncle killed his father, then married his mother. So he's hiding as best he can, despite the enormity of the secret he carries, as he is talking to these self-acknowledged spies. He's also expressing his anguish. *The world's rotten. I'm rotten.* These are two separate and distinct statements. Part of what makes this play so powerful is this interaction between an afflicted man, and this awful world. The audience knows it's not the only world out there. But he doesn't.

The end of Act 2 shows perhaps the most remarkable of Hamlet's soliloquies. Hamlet not only offers what he's thinking, but the audience also sees him changing his mind. He starts off thinking how much passion the actor showed as he acted out his grief. Compared to Hamlet's own feelings at his father's murder, the actor seemed vulnerable to much emotion. "Am I a coward?" Hamlet asks. At first he seems to answer *yes I am.* But then, as he thinks more, since the only proof of his father's murder involves a supernatural source, which may deceive, he wants to be careful. Particularly because the Devil might be exploiting Hamlet, "Out of my weakness and my melancholy," he devises a way, with a little play, that he might see if Claudius acts like a guilty man. The audience witnesses Hamlet's internal struggle as he tries to weigh all these factors, some of which involve his own afflictions.

ACT 3

At the very start of Act 3, Claudius and the gang, Gertrude, Polonius, Rosencrantz, and Guildenstern, are buzzing about why Hamlet seems not in his right mind. These aren't psychiatrists pondering what diagnosis and treatment might best benefit a patient. They want to know how dangerous this young man might prove to be. Claudius might just have him killed on the general principle that if Hamlet isn't dangerous now, he might become so. But it's complicated. Hamlet's family. Wouldn't have stopped Stalin. Uncle Joe killed off most of the top brass of the Soviet military in the years preceding Hitler's invasion, almost fatally crippling his country's ability to fend off the huge German onslaught. He believed the threat of a coup from his own generals was greater. Those who operate in a world where they perceive threats everywhere seem to have difficulty with their priorities.

Claudius does confirm what so far only the ghost has told us. The audience gets its proof of Claudius' crime ahead of Hamlet. His "deed" is a "heavy burden," the king says directly to us. He has to tell someone. Why not the audience, who by custom intend to just sit there and listen, no matter what? After this one admission, the audience no longer merely watches a play about a man told by his ghost father to avenge, etc., etc. It's a contest. The audience is to decide. Claudius wants the audience's sympathy. If it feels his pain, maybe it might have some ability to dissuade Hamlet from acting. Poor Claudius, so anguished, so alone with his guilt. Claudius' admission makes the audience part of the play, not mere onlookers. Its silence implicates it.

Roping the audience in helps set up Hamlet's pondering about action itself, his "to be or not to be . . ." that's gotten such notice over the centuries. The question for him isn't to act, or not to act. He's claiming humans create their existence in their actions. To be [a killer], or not to be [a killer] . . . that's the choice. *Who am I going to be?* Unlike all these others, Fortinbras, and shortly Laertes, Hamlet feels some capacity to ponder the course of his life. Contemporary audiences ought to appreciate this as a radical new notion for Shakespeare's original audience. Identity doesn't come from what an individual believes, or who the parents are, but rather from the actions taken in the world.

"Slings and arrows of outrageous fortune," he says. His particular *fortune* means killing the king. He quickly conflates that killing with his own death. He understands his action means his death. Hamlet doesn't have an army to protect him if he kills Claudius. When he does the deed at the end of the play, all shout "Treason! Treason!" This he knows. Hamlet's both suicidal in his own psyche, and understands acting on dad's command means he's equally dead.

But Hamlet abstracts all this in his speech. His list of a "sea of troubles" include aging, "the whips and scorns of time"; slave masters, "oppressor's wrong; jerks, "the proud man's contumely"; being dumped, "the pangs of despised love"; slow courts, "the law's delay"; and all insults, "the spurns that patient merit of the unworthy takes." He's wanting the listeners to understand his particular difficulty by offering a list of life's problems. Like Claudius, he's involving the audience in the drama. He wants those who hear him to identify with him, be on his side. He wants to gloss over how extraordinary, how unique, his particular *sea* truly is.

For most people, most of the time, *taking arms* doesn't involve traveling to the *undiscovered country*. People may have to go to the doctor or the physical therapist more often as they age, or quit their job, find a new lover, or a better lawyer, or just give some jerk the finger. For Hamlet, though, his *taking arms* involves his death. Does "conscience make cowards of us all?" Not really. Not even for Hamlet. He hesitates to kill Claudius, not for any feeling that this might be immoral, but because of its consequences for his life. He doesn't talk of some scruples that murder is wrong. He does understand, by the way he formulates the issue, that killing Claudius will seal his own fate. He lets listeners know he can't be impulsive about such an action. *As I think about it, a whole lot of me doesn't want this life*, he says. But he can't really get that far, clearly and articulately, in his formulation of it. He can only call himself a coward because he thinks too much.

"And lose the name of action," he concludes. But he is indeed *acting*. He's evaluating whether he wants to enter this world and what his chance of survival in it might be, how much his madness might be altering his perceptions, whether the Ghost is the Devil. He might from the beginning react with scorn and contempt for his uncle and his mother, but he's appreciating his choice of what to do about the Ghost's information and command for the complicated issue it is. He's in a context where no one else approaches the world this way. There's not much room for nuance in a kill-or-be-killed world. He's strikingly isolated.

And his lover turns out to be a spy. She's helping her father and his boss find out if he's a threat to their power. He seems to have some sense of this, as he asks her "Are you honest?" His scorn becomes understandable. Following daddy's orders, she breaks up with him. But she doesn't have a clue about how deeply Hamlet, and she, are in danger in this contest for state power. Hamlet's "get thee to a nunnery" isn't only the anger of a jilted lover. He's telling her *get out of here*. This world may destroy us both.

In the Kenneth Branaugh film version, a slight noise precedes Hamlet's question, "Where is your father?" By that sound, he knows Polonius and Claudius are listening. She's set him up. This helps explain Hamlet's deepening rage, as he fully lets in how much she's betraying him, even if it is somewhat unwittingly done. He curses her, giving her "this plague for thy dowry." He experiences a complicated mix of feelings. He's heartbroken, he's disgusted, but he counsels her to flee.

What's so amazing and delightful about many moments in this play, and why there's such a fuss about Shakespeare, comes vividly in Ophelia's reaction to Hamlet after he stalks off. She may be a naive fool, as she betrays her lover. She has no understanding of his plight or why he is so upset. But Ophelia's words of deep grief at her sense that there's tragedy here ring true. "Oh what a noble mind is here o'erthrown!" she laments. "Oh, woe is me, To have seen what I have seen, see what I see!" She may mistake the cause, but the emotions express the play's excruciating sadness.

To emphasize how Ophelia is merely a tool, as the king and her father re-enter, there's no recognition of her expression of feeling the audience has just heard. Claudius declares he's arranging to have Hamlet *sent to England*. In some versions of the play, Polonius snaps his head around at that phrase.

He understands this means Hamlet will be executed. "What think you on 't?" Claudius asks his counselor. "It shall do well," Polonius responds. He pushes for one more spying expedition, in Gertrude's bedroom, but if that doesn't work, well, "To England send him, or confine him where your wisdom best shall think." In *The Departed,* the Jack Nicholson character, the head of a Boston crime syndicate, tells an associate, "I got where I am today because I killed a lot of people."

Shakespeare ends this powerful scene with a nice little couplet:

It shall be so.
Madness in great ones must not unwatched go. (Act 3, scene 1, lines 195–96)

Unfortunately for this king, the great-one-with-the-army, Fortinbras, doesn't seem to have attracted anywhere near as much scrutiny. Because they can't figure him out, Hamlet's dangerous. Hamlet, raised in this environment, understands that this disguise affords him the best chance to hide.

Then Claudius gets upset at seeing the murder re-enacted on the stage and stalks off. Hamlet gets his proof. Scorns Rosencrantz and Guildenstern, ". . . do you think I am easier to be played on than a pipe?" Makes Polonius look foolish one last time. Then tells the audience of his resolve, "Now could I drink hot blood . . ." Maybe.

He comes upon Claudius, expressing to the audience, or God, which for Elizabethans is the same silent presence, how conscience-stricken he feels. He tries to pray. Hamlet seems set to slaughter him. He demurs. Reasons that he'd only send Claudius to heaven. But the same logic that the audience just heard Claudius express, the conundrum that

"Forgive me my foul murder" [he imagines praying]
That cannot be, since I am still possessed
Of those effects for which I did the murder—
My crown, mine own ambition, and my Queen. (Act 3, scene 3, lines 55-2-55)

This logic was just as evident to Hamlet. Couldn't Hamlet have inquired, *will you make a complete confession to everyone that you killed my father, and face execution for regicide?* Simple question. If Claudius replies *yes,* no need for Hamlet to interfere with justice. It would have been Claudius who would have been killed for his crime. If *no,* Hamlet can then send his uncle straight to hell. Either way, Hamlet will have fulfilled his father's Ghost's command. This is a win-win situation. Hamlet rejects it. He'll kill him when he's *drunk,* or *gambling,* or *having sex.* Claudius murdered his brother. The only way he can save his soul from going to hell involves his confession and death. After Hamlet leaves, Claudius gives up the praying, realizing he's not willing to give up what he's gained. *There's no such thing as heaven or hell,* a contemporary audience might even hear him muttering.

Hamlet, at this crucial moment, when the deed was there for the doing, doesn't want to enter into this world of murder and constant threat. He knows Claudius did it for sure. He had opportunity. His reasoning to demur is shallow and phoney. He doesn't want to be involved in this world this way. He soon changes his mind.

There in his mother's bedroom, he finds his passion. His rage and heartbreak cause him to become unhinged. He threatens his mother, such that she cries out in fear, "Thou wilt not murder me?" Hamlet stabs Polonius, thinking it was Claudius. His first act of murder doesn't slow him down very much. In fact, it shows how little he cares about the murdered, calling Polonius a "foolish, prating knave." He goes on to terrorize his mother. Rather than convinced by Hamlet, in the face of his deranged behavior, she has no choice but to act as if he's convincing her to comply with his demands.

In this serious discussion of the scene, there may be a moment to pause, and have a bit of fun with students. As the off-the-hook son berates his mom for leading her own life, in his fury he tells her,

Have you eyes?
You cannot call it love, for at your age,
The heyday in the blood is tame, it's humble,
And waits upon the judgment. (Act 3, scene 4, lines 67–69)

This depicts Hamlet as quite a young man, who knows nothing of the uncontrollable sexual passions of middle-aged people. Would students wish to be told more of their parents' unbridled sexual behavior? Never have they replied in the affirmative. They're very happy to get back to the play.

The Ghost reappears, only to Hamlet, serving to get him focused on Claudius, and leave his mother alone, as the Ghost had initially demanded of Hamlet. Quite a great old man you've got there, Hamlet. Cares a lot about you hurting his former wife, unsentimental-at-best as she might be. Doesn't seem to mind how laying on the revenge-task will destroy you. This warrior-hero dad was probably quite disappointed at his sensitive, thoughtful, depressed son. And come to think of it, if dad was so intent on revenge, why didn't he appear to Claudius, when he was praying? That might have fixed his wagon. Poor Hamlet. To everyone in the play, he's just a thing.

Had Hamlet been in his right mind, and possessing a contemporary consciousness, might he have said, *Dad. You want me to destroy myself, is that it? You want me to commit regicide? What's in it for me?* This is the tragedy. People now think this way. He could not.

ACT 4

Claudius sends him to England, this being a way to get rid of this dangerous person in a political way.

How dangerous is it that this man goes loose!
Yet must not we put the strong law on him.
He's loved of the distracted multitude,
Who like not in their judgment but their eyes . . . (Act 4, scene 3, lines 2–5)

    At the end of the scene he tells the audience directly, ahead of Hamlet's reporting to Horatio, that *sending to England* means death. He knows he can trust the audience to keep a secret.

    Hamlet sees Fortinbras' forces. This huge army travels across Denmark to contest a tiny bit of Poland. Hamlet finds this amazing and instructive. A good leader, he reflects, is able to motivate his soldiers to die for some trivial thing. He resolves

from this time forth,
My thoughts be bloody, or be nothing worth! (Act 4, scene 4, lines 65–66)

    This is all rather odd. Even he, seeing Fortinbras' soldiers, doesn't seem to think perhaps there may be more involved than a chunk of Poland. And his resolution to be *bloody*? A little late, isn't it? You're under guard, being transported to another country. He reveals himself to be quite an ordinary guy, way out of his depth in this contest for state power. The sense of doom increases, as the audience sits helplessly and watches this play out.

    Ophelia, having no good sense to get to a nunnery, does all that a helpless human being can do. She goes really mad. Finds her only true comfort there in the water. If it is fully comprehended how awful this world is, for her and Hamlet, her portrayal in this scene breaks the heart. She, like Hamlet, can't achieve, or even imagine, a life for themselves outside this specific world context.

    Before Laertes enters, full of fury at his father's killing, someone from the court reports that the people wish to proclaim Laertes to be king. This confirms again the low regard the people of Denmark have for their Current Occupant. Laertes displays what a son's vengeance ought to look like, full on.

To this point I stand,
That both the world I give to negligence.
Let come what comes, only I'll be revenged
Most thoroughly for my father. (Act 4, scene 5, lines 133–36)

Claudius uses much wiliness to divert Laertes from challenging his power. He explains how he had to send Hamlet away, rather than killing him for the murder, because of Hamlet's political popularity. The king's counting on Hamlet being executed in England, so that he might mollify Laertes, yet not be blamed for the death. Claudius seems adept at the close-in fighting, even if he's out to lunch about the threat Fortinbras poses.

When Claudius gets the note from Hamlet that he's returning from England, Claudius shifts into a plot to have Laertes kill Hamlet, in a duel. Here again, the king thinks like a crafty, if small-minded, politician. He seeks to have the deed done, without being the perpetrator.

Ophelia drowns herself. No one thought to watch this demented soul, just let her go on her own way? It must be concluded her *madness* could go *unwatched* since she wasn't *great*. She didn't count. She could be ignored.

ACT 5

Send in the clowns. The audience needs a break. All this grief requires some distraction. *It's only a play . . . . We're here to be entertained . . . . These people aren't like us.* The playwright wishes both to involve the audience in these terrible doings, and then to allow it to pull away, recover a sense of separateness, before he crushes the world it is watching/witnessing/participating in.

The gravediggers' work, as the riddle says, endures until the end of time. Given that the historical bones of another Shakespearean protagonist, King Richard III, were recently discovered beneath a parking lot, maybe the longevity of their work is exaggerated. But compared to all the mad, furious, tortured souls the audience has seen, these jokers, happy at their work, are quite a relief.

Hamlet returns. It all seems so normal. Perhaps he's back from a business trip? It's only when the magnitude of his decision to show up in Denmark is considered that the question comes: *why?* He was free. He could have bribed the pirates who picked him up on the high seas to drop him anywhere. He might have written to Horatio, said *meet me in Wittenberg. Bring money.* He might have seen if he could ally with Fortinbras to bring down Claudius. Or used his popularity, appreciated even by Claudius, on his own to attempt to overthrow the Current Occupant. Instead, he makes his reappearance, unarmed, no army, to embrace his own doom. This is what gives such poignance to the graveyard scene. Hamlet feels he'll be joining Yorick and all the others soon.

Given the way they parted, Hamlet's protestations at Ophelia's burial might seem histrionic. Certainly Laertes' display ought to be viewed this way. But this gives Hamlet an opportunity to express his true grief for everything that's happened, and will continue to happen, in front of mom and Claudius. The king doesn't have Hamlet put under guard directly, only admonishing Gertrude to "Put some watch over your son." He understands he must dispose of Hamlet by stealth.

Hamlet's sense of doom finds expression in his telling Horatio,

There's a divinity that shapes our ends,
Roughhew them how we will. (Act 5, scene 2, lines 10–11)

But this isn't true. The last three hundred years of human thought since the Enlightenment proclaims freedom as central to existence. Human life isn't determined by a God, or by a Church, or a king or slave masters. That's what *life, liberty and the pursuit of happiness* mean. Human beings may act to create their own *fate*. Philosophers, poets, playwrights, novelists, armies, all have struggled to imagine and achieve this sense of *freedom*. Hamlet finds himself trapped in an intellectual world prior to this revolution in human thinking. Ultimately, he had no conceptual framework to envision another way of living.

Hamlet must know the duel ends it. There may be some treachery. He knows Laertes wants his revenge. Claudius had previously given orders to have him killed. This clever young man, knowing who his enemies are, might never even have had a chance to get at Claudius after all, but for the happenstance of the swords being exchanged. Claudius and Laertes would have gotten what they wanted. Despite his eloquent anguish, his soulful pondering, the duel and its aftermath seem so pathetic and tawdry, yet so poignant.

Gertrude has her moment. Some directors, with glances and pauses as Claudius warns her, "Do not drink!" make her drinking seem knowingly suicidal. Like Ophelia, she might presumably have had enough of all this, wish to take her quietus. It's what folks do, when they feel trapped. She might imagine her son will soon die. She doesn't want to witness this.

Hamlet, not having much life left in him, finally has the opportunity in the chaos to take care of his father's business. "The rest is silence," only for him.

Horatio's send off, as Hamlet dies in his arms

Now cracks a noble heart. Good night,
sweet Prince,
And flights of angels sing thee to thy rest! (Act. 5, scene 2, lines 369–71)

These words were so powerful and effective when Martin Luther King, Jr., borrowed them to characterize the children killed in the Birmingham church bombing. Horatio's sorrow feels genuine. His dear friend was caught in a world not of his making. There may be some skittishness about going all the way with *noble heart.* The way he talks to and about his mother, or Ophelia, or his complete surrender to his doom, suggest he's no more *noble* than other humans, stuck in their lives with limited imaginations and restricted views of other people. In death, he seems much more as part of humanity, one who tried, and failed.

This view gets reinforced by the very next thing Horatio says. He lies. In reply to the English ambassador's query, "Where should we have our thanks?" Horatio informs him, "He never gave commandment for their [Rosencrantz and Guildenstern's] death." The audience heard Hamlet tell Horatio he had given exactly that order. Furthermore, Hamlet didn't care. "They [Rosencrantz and Guildenstern] are not near my conscience," he tells his friend. Without Hamlet to protect him, Horatio has to fend for himself in this vicious world. Better to push the blame away from Hamlet, onto Claudius. This will help maintain the image of the *sweet prince,* as the power now shifts to Fortinbras. The spin just keeps on spinning.

Fortinbras can't believe his good fortune. All his enemies have killed each other, like Quentin Tarantino's ending to *Reservoir Dogs*. The Current Occupant, Fortinbras' father's killer's son, the wife of the two previous kings, even the king's advisor's son, all done away with. Most directors have Fortinbras sit down, as he's speaking, and put on the crown. *Lah-di-dah. That was easy.* With one last little bit of politicking, Fortinbras gives directions to have Hamlet, but not Claudius, honored as a *soldier.* "For he was likely, had he been put on, to have proved most royally."

There's no evidence in the play Hamlet was any sort of *soldier*. Hamlet knows, juxtaposed to Fortinbras, he wasn't much of a military leader. Fortinbras seemed to intuit that Hamlet, unlike Claudius, did seem to have had people who felt affection toward him. Since his potential rival Hamlet was dead, might as well curry favor with his supporters with a nice funeral.

One recent version of the play has Fortinbras taking out his pistol, when he says, "Go, bid the soldiers shoot," and firing into Horatio's head. That may be a bit over the top, going farther than the playwright intended, but it does underscore the ruthlessness of this world. Humankind has come a long way, with democracies, *inalienable rights,* respect for law. This play abides so deeply in the collective consciousness because it stands as a reminder of what remains only among drug traffickers, crime syndicates, despotic governments. The audience leaves the theater feeling gratitude that Elsinor, while lurking in the shadows of the modern world, isn't the *prison* humans inhabit.

Talking about literature means talking about what is in human consciousness right now. If students can take in the great agony portrayed in this play, if their stomachs inform them they've witnessed a *tragedy,* they might cherish the current world, its freedoms, its protections, its real choices. Perhaps that's Shakespeare's abiding gift. And why, if teachers and students persist and engage with the actual play, it is honored so highly.

Chapter 16

How can this Murderer
Be Understood?

Reading: *Crime and Punishment* by Fyodor Dostoevsky, translated by
Richard Pevear and Larissa Volokhonsky

And with this tortured, terrible young man, how can anyone make sense of
what he has done? There are two main ways.

The first is through a philosophical/historical lens. Raskolnikov might be
viewed as a prototype of the radical intellectual of that time and place. He's
responding to the evident human suffering he sees all around him in the mid-
nineteenth-century Russian city of St. Petersburg. There certainly were lots of
nasty, brutish, and short[1] human lives being lived there. There was no social
safety net, no sense that starving children were anyone's problem but of their
parents. People of conscience ached but could do nothing in a totalitarian,
rigid class society.

Russia was a country where almost 40 percentage of the population was
held in bondage to the land. They were called *serfs* although the difference
between them and American *slaves* wasn't much. It was a system, like
America's, held in place with much violence and collusion on the part of the
church and the social structure. It made some very rich, everyone else quite
poor. Think of Bangladesh or Haiti today. Those who cared about the fate of
human beings raged about this state of the people, dreamed of a better world,
by any means necessary.

Raskolnikov thought he'd be doing a good thing, killing the pawnbroker,
taking her money, giving it to help the poor. She exploited poor people. The
world, he decided, would be better off without her. He was willing to take on
the moral burden of murder, to prove he was a person capable of such decisions, an *extraordinary man,* not bound to the usual ideas that prohibited the
taking of life. He'd be like Napoleon, living above such moral restrictions.

In this philosophical/historical view, Raskolnikov's struggle in the novel comes from trying to live up to this image of himself. When he can't, and he confesses, the failure isn't of his philosophy, but rather of him as its instrument. His friend Razumikhin, with his devotion to Raskolnikov when he's ill, his lover Sonya, with her emphasis on the dictates of the human heart, and his police pursuer Porfiry, with his insistence on the rule of law, are arrayed against him. They in their fashion assert a different philosophy that emphasizes the humanity of every individual. By the very end of the novel, in the epilogue, Raskolnikov gets closer to Sonya's views. He hasn't embraced them yet, but the reader might imagine that he does. His falling in love with Sonya is his beginning of connecting to all of humanity.

Raskolnikov's final dream in the epilogue might be considered a prescient view of the horrors of the first half of the twentieth century.

> Some new trichinae had appeared, microscopic creatures that lodged themselves in men's bodies. But these creatures were spirits, endowed with reason and will. Those who received them into themselves immediately became possessed and mad. But never, never had people considered themselves so intelligent and unshakable in the truth as did these infected ones. Never had they thought their judgments, their scientific conclusions, their moral convictions and beliefs more unshakeable. Entire settlements, entire cities and nations would be infected and go mad. Everyone became anxious, and no one understood anyone else; each thought the truth was contained in himself alone, and suffered looking at others, beat his breast, wept, and wrung his hands. They did not know whom or how to judge, could not agree to accuse, whom to vindicate. People killed each other in some sort of meaningless spite. (p. 546)

But all this is known. These philosophical ideas, so prominent in the nineteenth century, turned the twentieth century into a disaster. Raskolnikov's image of Napoleon as an example of an *extraordinary man* pales in comparison with the twentieth century's Hitler, Stalin, Mao, Pol Pot, Milosevic. Perhaps even the George W. Bush administration official should be included.

> We're an empire now, and when we act, we create our own reality. And while you're studying that reality—judiciously, as you will—we'll act again, creating other new realities, which you can study too, and that's how things will sort out. We're history's actors . . . and you, all of you, will be left to just study what we do.[2]

This echoes the philosophical notion that claimed for a government and its military the right to kill for an idea.

Our current human-rights movement attempts to fulfill Dostoevsky's vision of a world composed of individual human beings, above all. But what gives this novel such power doesn't come only from this prophetic portrayal of the fate of these philosophical notions.

People also keep reading and thinking about this book because it depicts someone who kills, he says, for an idea. This deadly phenomenon still hasn't been figured out. Some young brothers leave bombs at the finish line of the Boston Marathon. No one has a clue why they might do this. It can perhaps be grasped that deranged people took lives at a grade school in Connecticut, or at a high school in Colorado, but murders like those in Boston, or in nineteenth-century St. Petersburg seem more calculating and detached, and thus inexplicable. Dostoevsky offers the opportunity to get inside the head of such a killer.

Such a view starts with the notion that *for Raskolnikov the desire to kill comes first.* He then invents reasons, philosophies, goals for the deed. If he had been really interested in doing something political, or even socially revolutionary, shouldn't he have killed a banker, or rich landowner, or a particularly noisome government official? There certainly were lots to choose from. The pawnbroker and her unfortunate sister were merely convenient.

Consider what havoc the Boston Marathon bombers might have caused, going through city after city, subways, buses, athletic events, with their backpacks, if they were genuinely interested in bringing the sorrows of their people to America. They might have gone a month or two without apprehension. Instead, after their first bombing, they went home and had dinner. It might be a lack of imagination or gumption, which the world is grateful for. But their heart, like Raskolnikov's, wasn't in their philosophical intent. They wanted to kill some people, for the thrill, the sense of dominance arising from their alienation. They had in themselves some bit of the monster that sought expression in the world. Some people set out to climb a mountain, others to write a book, others to find a cure for disease.

Raskolnikov's intention was an ambition, which he then found reasons to justify.

The novel then becomes a struggle between reconciling this monstrousness with the claims of humanity. Unlike those who kill with no feeling of remorse, from military leaders to serial killers, Raskolnikov, like Hamlet and Sethe, is split into elements of both monster and human. This is evident in Raskolnikov's first dream, where he witnesses, from a child's view, a horse being beaten to death by its drunken enraged owner. Raskolnikov wakes from the dream resolving to not commit the foul deed he has planned. Then he does the killing anyway. Even more, the younger and completely innocent sister comes upon him in the act, and he kills her too.

Raskolnikov lives in the world of other human beings. He has relations with them. When he falls into a delirium after the killings, his friend Razumikhin takes care of him. He becomes involved with Sonya, a lovely young woman, whose soul is untouched by her prostitution. It's clear Raskolnikov wants a human life. He's not just a monster.

However, he doesn't want his monster to get caught. He evades the police, lies to them, tries to keep the knowledge of his terrible deeds to himself. His evading punishment is what would prove to him that he wasn't a monster. According to his vision of what ought to be, he had acted rationally. Much like Sethe claiming "Schoolteacher ain't got 'em" as a way to justify her actions long after her murder of her child, Raskolnikov defends his madness. If he were to say to himself "I was crazy," this would be abandoning this part of himself. It would not heal the split, but it would mean he'd have to live without this part of himself. It would lead to the kind of grief we saw when Beloved ran away from Sethe. "I lost my best thing," she tells Paul D.

Marmeladov and Svidrigailov portray two other characters who struggle with their monstrousness. Marmeladov prostitutes his daughter to support his drinking and his family. Svidrigailov, having killed his first wife, plots to marry Raskolnikov's sister. It would seem both come to awareness of their evil. They both take actions, Marmeladov by walking in front of a galloping horse and carriage, Svidrigailov by shooting himself, that display one way of contending with the split Raskolnikov struggles with. But Raskolnikov wants to live.

He fights detection with everything in him. Only when his alienation from all those around him becomes too painful, when mother, sister, friend, lover, even Porfiry, beckon him back to humanity, does he find a way. Sonya's notion that he killed a human being finally penetrates his psyche. He confesses, but only as I-tried-and-failed-to-be-extraordinary. Only his enduring connection with Sonya in a Siberian prison allows him to begin to abandon this justification. After much deprivation and suffering, as Porfiry claims,

I'm sure you'll decide to embrace suffering . . . Because suffering . . . is a great thing . . . There is an idea in suffering. (p. 461)

Raskolnikov by the end is only coming to this awareness that he wasn't *weak,* or that there's no such thing as *extraordinary men.* All that is real are individual human beings. This is not a philosophical understanding, but rather a feeling from the heart, as Sonya shows us. The monster can't be made rational. It must be separated from what is truly human.

A solely philosophical view of the novel, excluding this psychological perspective, might provide fuel for his demented murderousness. It would lend credence to his monster/human split, as if there really were *extraordinary men.* Raskolnikov just wasn't one of them. A better understanding of Dostoevsky's novel would be to assert that Napoleon-Hitler-Stalin-Mao and all the others were demented power-hungry sadists, not human beings. The philosophy Raskolnikov struggles throughout much of the novel to incorporate into human life, and also all these other ideologies, from National Socialism to the Dictatorship of the Proletariat to Mao's Little Red Book, were all ways to justify their murderous cruelty.

NOTES

1. "And the life of man, solitary, poore, nasty, brutish, and short." Seventeenth century British philosopher Thomas Hobbes, in his treatise, *Leviathan.*

2. From an October 17, 2004, *The New York Times Magazine* article by writer Ron Suskind, quoting an unnamed aide to George W. Bush (later attributed, by journalist Mark Danner, to Karl Rove).

Chapter 17

A Portrait of a Middle-Aged Woman and a Madman, in London, in 1923

Reading: *Mrs. Dalloway* by Virginia Woolf.

A lovely, wonderful book, although sometimes too high a threshold for a portion of the students. Some years it doesn't get assigned, if it's judged it will go unread by too large a percentage. But if there are enough who might persist past the difficulties created as Virginia Woolf gets into the heads of her characters, it's given a go.

There's a comprehension struggle, since readers find themselves, with no background information, immediately inside the thoughts of Clarissa Dalloway as she's preparing for her party that night. Readers need patience to contend with knowing little about what's going on. The perspective, even the story itself, shifts from one character or scene to another without an indication that this has happened. Reading requires close attention despite the reader mainly feeling bewildered. Those unfamiliar with Woolf's approach, termed stream of consciousness, although it's more like a lake, will need to endure for maybe a third of the book before it starts to make much sense, or feels like they're being told a story.

The felt experience of reading this book for students might be like being on an airplane where they can hear the thoughts of every passenger. They are given no context, no sense of who is speaking. They just hear passengers thinking. At first, this might be confusing and disturbing. But after a while, the listener might become absorbed in these private, secret recollections, ponderings, regrets of the passengers.

It's also an interest-challenge, at least in the early going, particularly with Clarissa. She's a middle-aged wife and mother putting all her energy into a party. She reflects on her life, the people she likes and those she doesn't, the choices she's made. Although she has a teenage daughter, the thoughts and feelings of this British woman married to a government official from almost a hundred years ago may not be all that compelling to high school students. They initially find her a snotty, cold, silly person.

The other focus of the novel, Septimus Smith, can be downright scary to behold. He's going quite crazy. His portrayal may repel readers.

The novel offers many rewards if readers persist through these difficulties. The satisfaction of reading the book will be getting to know the main characters, Clarissa Dalloway and Septimus Smith. Clarissa emerges as a thoughtful, sensitive, reflective person with much substance. The portrayal of Septimus' descent into madness can be moving as it draws readers into his, and his wife's, agony. A possible definition of good fiction might be when readers find themselves feeling closer to people conjured on the page than most if not all of the actual people in their own lives. But the novel requires a fairly deep level of surrender, to both its form and content. Some years a fairly large number of students do this.

The first reward becomes a sense of the close connection of a character's consciousness to the world and its troubles. Knowing Clarissa acquaints young people with how it felt to be alive immediately after the Great War:

> This late age of the world's experience had bred in them all, all men and women, a well of tears. Tears and sorrows; courage and endurance; a perfectly upright and stoical bearing. Think, for example, of the woman she admired the most, Lady Bexborough, opening the bazaar. (p. 9)

Part of the challenge of the book lies in not knowing, at that early point in the novel, what there was to admire about Lady Bexborough's action. Only later do readers understand that she had just learned her son had been killed in battle. Despite her grief, she performed her civic duty, presiding at the opening of a shopping area, to express her determination to preserve a sense of civilization and community.

So even Clarissa, at some distance from the events of her world's recent history, felt the agony of the time. The novel occurs on a very specific day, June 15, 1923. Grief abounded in the world. An awareness of the world's darkness transforms her efforts to have a successful party into an assertion of life. Young people ought to acquire this sense of the struggle against the grief in human events.

As she reflects on her life, Clarissa displays that regret or reexamination of life's choices can't be avoided. Should she have married the dashing, witty Peter Walsh rather than the steady but maybe not really fun guy she did? Did she make some mistakes allowing her daughter to be involved with the raging, spiteful Miss Kilman? She ponders the path of her life, what she decided to do, and not do, what she fell into, or what she didn't know was important.

She encourages all the students to ponder how legitimate it may be to have an inner life, even if it might be vastly different than what they present to the world. Getting inside Clarissa's head, where readers hear her kind and petty thoughts, her affection for her daughter and her husband, her hatred for Miss Kilman and others, helps liberate a reader's own secret inner life.

Readers might understand how life decisions, even twenty years later, aren't necessarily without ambiguity. Clarissa still ponders her decision about marrying Richard. Was it the right one? Maybe. For young people, on the cusp of making many life decisions, Clarissa's self-examination might console them. They may not be able to avoid regrets, reexaminations. This is part of living, her thoughts suggest.

The novel also suggests to students, particularly those who didn't much care for Clarissa, that people do not look all that lovely if others could hear their innermost thoughts. Petty, nasty, small, creepy notions occur to all. Humans have learned to keep them inside, unspoken. Humility is needed as readers contemplate Clarissa, given the uncensored access readers have to her mind.

Reading Clarissa's thoughts helps readers realize how separate she is from those around her. With her reactions to these other people, her husband, her daughter, her dear friend Sally, that she'd never say to them, Woolf involves the reader with a full and complicated human being, not someone defined by her role as wife or mother or friend. Given the times, and the misogynistic world she inhabits, this portrayal of her humanity becomes in itself a feminist statement, an assertion of her worth.

It's through Peter Walsh, her former sweetheart and imagined alternate life, that readers get some of the powerful ways Clarissa exists in the world, despite the sorrow, even the loss of her dear sister to an accidental death.

> As we are a doomed race, chained to a sinking ship, . . . as the whole thing is a bad joke, let us, at any rate, do our part: mitigate the sufferings of our fellow-prisoners . . .; decorate the dungeon with flowers and air-cushions; be as decent as we possibly can. Those ruffians, the Gods, shan't have it all their own way,—her notion being that the Gods, who never lost a chance of hurting, thwarting and spoiling human lives were seriously put out if, all the same, you behaved like a lady. (p. 76)

By the end of the novel, even the seemingly random juxtapositions of her with Septimus make sense.

> So that to know her, or any one, one must seek out the people who completed them; even the places. Odd affinities she had with people she had never spoken to, some woman in the street, some man behind a counter—even trees, or barns.

It ended in a transcendental theory which, with her horror of death, allowed her to believe, or say that she believed (for all her scepticism), that since our apparitions, the part of us which appears, are so momentary compared with the other, the unseen part of us, which spreads wide, the unseen might survive, be recovered somehow attached to this person that, or even haunting certain places after death . . . perhaps—perhaps. (p. 149)

Clarissa emerges as a person with a mystical awareness, suggesting the existence of a pattern where readers initially only saw chaos. Through this character, Virginia Woolf gives much to wonder about as readers walk down a city street.

Septimus Smith might be less disturbing if he were a portrait from the past of someone whose affliction can now be cured. But people might encounter today a poor soul suffering with such Post Traumatic Stress Disorder. While such sufferers can now be sedated far more effectively than in the England of the1920s, as can be seen with the recent shootings much in the news, the violent, destructive psychosis evident in Septimus still lies largely beyond the ability to prevent or cure. His agony, and that of his wife, persist in the contemporary world. Loved ones still slip from reality into hallucinations. They leave those around them equally helpless.

Doctors seem more humble now, compared with those who tried to treat Septimus. But today's public vilifies a mentally ill person with the same vehemence, even if there may be the notion of PTSD causing the illness, rather than the weak will, or low intelligence. Yet, the tragedy portrayed in his suicide abides with many of the soldiers, returning from Iraq and Afghanistan. Septimus' story is painful to read, particularly juxtaposed against Clarissa's middle-class ethos. If readers can nevertheless do so, they will perhaps share a bit of some of the returning soldiers' pain.

There are two smaller arguments about the novel to be made. These often evoke great interest in discussion. Clarissa was right in not marrying Peter Walsh. Richard Dalloway was a far better mate to her, despite her musing at one point early on,

If I had married him, this gaity would have been mine all day! (p. 46)

Their attraction to each other was so romantic, students protest. Richard is so dull, so preoccupied with his work. Ah, but what is his work? He turns out to be a human-rights advocate even before such a term or occupation existed. His perspective perhaps became an inspiration for Amnesty International. He cares about the fate of the Armenians and the Albanians, both of whom were slaughtered during The Great War.

As a member of the British government, Richard was doing his best to sound the alarm, make the world know of the atrocities being committed. When Hitler contemplated The Final Solution, the Fuhrer wrote, "Who, after all, speaks today of the annihilation of the Armenians?" Clarissa loved and cared for a very good man. In this way, Richard Dalloway compares well to Peter, who shows up the day of the party as a lost soul, having drifted about the British Empire, seducing a married woman, and never having done much with his lofty ideals.

Readers might also develop some understanding of, if not compassion for, Septimus' doctors, as horridly as they are portrayed. Yes, one of them does remark, "The coward!" (p. 146) when he hears of Septimus' suicide. But that was his ignorance talking, masked by his arrogance. These people knew absolutely nothing about what to do with a damaged, psychotic psyche. They had no medications, no concepts, no ability to contend at all with this full-blown madness. Yet, desperate loved ones begged them to do something. They may have forgotten they were putting on a show of effort, but at least these practitioners tried to contend with their own helplessness and that of others. Readers may scorn them, now, but some restraint is called for. Humanity's defenses against ignorance never look good.

So this novel, if students will allow for it, shows much about the intersection of history and art, of war and its grief, the agony of a damaged psyche. If students can make the climb, they will not be the same people after reading this novel.

Chapter 18

Now, Who's the Monster Here?

Reading: *Frankenstein,* 1818 Edition, by Mary Shelley.

What might be said about this old saw of a novel might seem more of a Jeremiad than a presentation of an analytical perspective. Such an amazing book. Traveling from the imagination of a nineteen-year-old young woman in the early nineteenth century, it now finds itself in the farthest reaches of the contemporary literary and pop culture, with Mary Shelley seminars, frankenfoods, and wooden pegs protruding from the neck of every monster at Halloween. So much about both the content of the book and the way it has been mistreated over the centuries could enrage a careful reader: the behavior of the title character Victor Frankenstein; the modern distortion of the sense of the novel; and the truth of how humans treat each other.

Victor Frankenstein? He's awful. He makes this creature. When it comes alive, and goes to him, yearning, beseeching his creator to embrace him, protect him and guide him in this strange world, Victor rejects him, runs away in horror. Mothers who do this are condemned. What motivates the creature to commit violence stems from his great hunger for what any human desires: affection, protection, instruction. Victor's total rejection of the creature breaks the reader's heart.

Victor remains silent as Justine, the poor young thing, gets executed for murdering Victor's brother William. Not once, but several times, he might have saved her life, telling the authorities she didn't do it, this creature that I made did. But noooo. Victor hides. Justine hangs.

All the creature wants is a female companion, a very human desire. Then he'll leave Victor's family alone. Victor initially agrees. He gets the creature's hopes up. It then occurs to Victor that these two might be fruitful and multiply. So Victor destroys the almost-finished mate to the creature. The enraged creature kills Victor's friend Henry, then Victor's new wife. Um, Victor, couldn't you just have left out the ovaries of the new gal?

In *The Annotated Frankenstein,* edited by Susan J. Wolfson and Ronald Levao, they consider that Victor was, in fact, quite mentally ill. That might be one way to have some empathy for this character. All that transpires would be products of his diseased mind. He is the one telling his story. He wants readers to understand he's not to blame. The difficulty of such a reading stems largely from everyone around him seeming to suffer far more than he does for his madness. He seems like the person who asks the judge for mercy as an orphan after having killed his parents.

Of all the characters portrayed in the novel, the creature himself emerges as the most fully human. Readers get to know his yearning, his rage, his education in the ways of the world. Like Bigger Thomas, his murders are reprehensible, yet they seem understandable as human acts. He's an outcast. No wonder he's raging and vengeful.

Especially as he tells of his overhearing about history with the De Lacys, readers have some feeling for his quick intelligence, even his empathy for the downtrodden, ". . . as he wept with Safie [the woman being told about history] over the hapless fate of the original inhabitants [of the Americas]." (p. 95) Victor's creation not only has a body able of superhuman endurance and speed. The creature's mind seems large, eager, able to quickly comprehend his surroundings. The story he tells of himself to Walton impresses with his sensitivity and articulateness.

Huck and Tom had last names, but Jim didn't. This ought to be understood as part of the denigration of an African-American slave. It signifies his less-than-human status in the white supremacist slave culture. Shelley's central character, fully human in aspect, doesn't even have a first name. Victor refers to him as the creature, the wretch, the monster, with none of the quality of personhood that even a first name conveys. He embodies all those nameless "ripped, and shucked and scattered" as Heaney might say. Readers shiver, as he sounds like Osama Bin Laden in his 9/11 message[1] after he kills William,

I, too, can create desolation; my enemy is not impregnable; this death will carry despair to him, and a thousand other miseries shall torment and destroy him. (p. 117)

Those who suffer seek to destroy their tormentors. They are the wretched of the earth, striving for redress. The privileged should not be surprised at how angry they are, how they rejoice at making misery. If readers can feel for this character in this work of fiction, such things might be understood.

It's quite instructive what happened to this tale once it made its way to Hollywood in the twentieth century. The articulate, thoughtful creature, whose revenge was quite specifically targeted to his creator's family, is transformed into a mute psychopath named . . . Frankenstein. Many people organize to kill him, not just Victor. Victor gets portrayed as daffy and goofy in a fuddy-duddy old-professor way, or as a power-hungry scientist, but not as someone who rejects his creation, since from the beginning all the creature does is pursue people to kill them. Readers are meant to identify not with the wretch, but with the more-human-appearing Victor.

Film versions thus deprive the creature of his voice and readers' ability to connect to him. He can't explain why he feels so mistreated, thus there's no empathy. Without seeing Victor shun his creation, there's no understandable human reason why the creature becomes violent. The creature only becomes this malevolent force intent on destruction. There's no link of the actions of other humans to his reaction. The creature in the films can't be reasoned with or placated. It isn't that his loneliness or alienation and consequent rage might make sense to us. The response to this force can only be to crush it.

Not since the character of Uncle Tom, a kind, brave, moral character in *Uncle Tom's Cabin*, became synonymous with a collaborating coward has there been such a complete reversal from the original work of art to the general cultural understanding.

The creature-as-Frankenstein, as an image in contemporary culture, seems to warn about science run amok. But in the novel it's not this creation that randomly causes pain that can't be controlled. It's the irresponsibility of the creator that begins the depredations. He could have acted to end the creature's threat. He might have gotten a gun and shot the creature. Or organized a group of people with guns to do the deed. It isn't Victor's arrogance at performing life science that brings him to grief. It's his rejection, even denial, of what he creates.

That's why Richard Wright named his book *Native Son*. He wanted readers to embrace Bigger Thomas as what a racist society generated. What happens in Mary Shelley's book isn't the fault of science. A father rejects his son. The son seeks revenge. The lesson, rather than a warning about the dangers of science, might be how crucial it is to love what people labor to produce. Hey Laius, you want to make sure your son doesn't kill you when he grows up? Love him, so that he loves you back, and is thus willing to leave his first love, his mother, and find his own woman.

And wouldn't America have been better off acknowledging Bin Laden as its creation? America trained and armed him when he fought the Soviet enemy in Afghanistan. He then turned his ferocity upon us. Should America have been so surprised? He and his colleagues took great offense to American economic and military might in his world. They even had declared war on the United States. Yet, Americans label them monsters or terrorists. If Americans had understood their connection to them, might the country have become aware how dangerous they were? Many died miserably, for lack of what America couldn't find there, to paraphrase William Carlos Williams' poem.

Despite all attempts to reduce or deny the power of this novel in the world, like any great work of art, it continues to disturb. It continues to be read and pondered. There's awe at what this nineteen-year-old young woman produced, there at the beginning of the modern world. She may have had some help from great literary minds, the poets Lord Byron and her husband Percy Shelley. But so do all artists. She put it together. It was her work.

It remains a prescient vision of the dynamics of oppression. However distorted movies and pop culture have made it, it originates from the artistic vision of a very young person. She may have come from a literary and dissident family. Dad was William Godwin, an eighteenth-century Norman Mailer perhaps, writer, rascal, public leftist intellectual. Mom was Betty Friedan's intellectual ancestor, Mary Wollstonecraft, writing one of the first books about feminism. Their daughter may have had a head start, but this only shows what might be possible for any young artist given the right conditions.

This gets pointed out to high school students, two or three years away from Mary Shelley's age when she wrote this novel. The intent isn't to diminish them, but rather to honor the creative possibilities of their young lives. Who knows what they might produce that will be meaningful for centuries? They ought never to allow any other people to curtail their imaginative power.

"Don't let anyone tell you differently," the creature might have said, to his real creator.

NOTE

1. "You who dropped a nuclear bomb on Japan, even though Japan was ready to negotiate an end to the war. How many acts of oppression, tyranny and injustice have you carried out, O callers to freedom?"

Chapter 19

An Engaged Intellectual, Caught Between Two Peoples

Readings: selections from *Once Upon a Country, A Palestinian Life* by Sari Nusseibeh and a review of the book by Amos Elon in *The New York Review of Books,* April 26, 2007.

This is an exposure to the Palestinian academic, philosopher, and activist, now the head of the Arab university in Jerusalem, Al-Quds University. As an example of an engaged intellectual, he can show students how art arises from these thinking people immersed in conflict. He's quite admirable: both jailed by the Israelis and beaten up by Palestinian fanatics. He offers a vision of the Israeli-Palestinian conflict where neither side has all the truth, or is in sole possession of all the good or evil. He wants Israelis and Palestinians to imagine the lives of the other side, as any true artist might.

Students read a thoughtful review of the book by a prominent Israeli journalist, and then some selections from the book itself. This allows students to have an encounter with the man and his thinking. Some percentage of students in the class are Jewish, a very few are Arab. The Jewish students remark that they've never read anything like what Nusseibeh has to say. My Arab students have liked a chance to talk about this conflict that weighs heavy on their hearts. So even this brief exposure can open up a new perspective, even liberate a classroom.

Nusseibeh shows how both sides of a political struggle may attack the moderates, since conflict itself rewards the extremes. One side can justify their violence, their disregard of law and the humanity of the other side, if all that exists are the extremists on the other side. Israeli and Palestinian hardliners can each point to the terrible things the other did. As Nusseibeh shows, there can be no resolution to this conflict without some understanding of the middle ground. He comments on the "second intifada" [violent uprising of the Palestinian people against Israeli rule in lands occupied after the 1967 war]:

> if the so-called "intellectual" of a society refuses to oppose misguided public opinion, either because he fears for his life or hopes for personal gain or popularity, then that "intellectual" has lost his role in society, and his society will be as lost as he is. (p. 429)

Nusseibeh observed that the Israelis and Palestinians ought not to view each other as enemies, but rather as allies. They are the only ones that share a mutual interest in the land and its outcome. The United States, a seemingly strong supporter of Israel, or the Arab allies of the Palestinians have their own domestic reasons for showing support to their side. Only those two peoples, who live on the land, care deeply about it and its future. But the Israelis will never succeed in crushing the Palestinian desire for freedom. The Palestinians will never remove Israel from the Middle East. They are stuck with each other. It would be far better if both sides understood how much their mutual interests coincide.

Nusseibeh talks of how the weaker fighter in a conflict often has more power to resolve it. They have less to lose. They're already restrained, conquered. They can change more easily. If the Palestinians were to renounce violence, he offers, they would be in a position to condemn the de-humanizing treatment by the Israelis without being dehumanized.

Big thoughts. Powerful thoughts. All a school-test can do is have students give back what Nusseibeh said from the readings. All a class discussion can do is begin a process of consideration. Such talk may open some eyes, allow minds to take in a new thought. But what can't be determined is how much a different way of thinking will be absorbed. Acquaintance with ideas is what can happen. Let it go at that.

Yet, this is what real education is about. It's a rubbing against real ideas that matters greatly in the world. It offers ways to think about human conflicts that seem intractable. While this is a long way from standardized-test bubbling-in, it is the work worth doing.

Chapter 20

Some Thoughts on Senioritis as an Environmental Disease and the Glories of a Hiatus in a Young Person's Life

It's a unique time for a human being, to be a second-semester senior in high school. There may be a way to re-imagine it, so that time doesn't become a travail for teachers, or their parents, or for young people themselves.

Consider what might be said by students, if they could travel back in time to speak to themselves as they were entering first grade. These little persons would, of course, be quite worried about this strange new situation. *Would I get into trouble, learn to read, remember the time tables, have any friends?* Any adult would attempt to be kind to the anxious children. The older person would encourage them *to try their best.* Saying, *it will be okay.*

If early school experiences proved to be painful for these children, a compassionate adult would strive to refocus their difficulties onto other causes that said less about them, and more about the context they find themselves in. An adult might say, *you aren't stupid. You just need to have this math broken down into smaller pieces.* Or, *the kid who makes you feel terrible does so because he's messed up, not you.* The role of someone with more experience in living would be to lighten the children's load, so that they might be able to enjoy themselves, feel their own power, there at the beginning of their school lives.

There may be a similar service a teacher might perform for young people at the closing of this high school chapter of their lives. A teacher might seek to liberate students from the shame associated with the dreaded disease of senioritis. This is where a formerly diligent student doesn't do homework, or show up for school that often, or care about school. Students may actually have been anticipating for quite some time this period of slacking off. Yet, very few of them can withstand the anxious or angry words or even a disapproving glance from teacher or parent. They hang their heads in shame. It may be partly a show, but some real pain or discord abides.

Consider that it may be possible for students to feel good about themselves in this last bit of their high school experience. There may be ways to equip them to have more informed and convincing discussions with people who consider them afflicted with senioritis.

Their condition doesn't require curing. Teachers might succeed though in putting their students' minds at ease. They may be able to teach students how to lead others to relax their anxious grip upon their young lives. Teachers could assist students to bask in the glories of this rare life event called a *hiatus*.

Students have spent the last several years, and particularly the last two, qualifying themselves for admission to college. In almost all cases, they have succeeded. Maybe not as much as they might wish, but it shall suffice. It would be useful for students to locate in themselves that sense of self-acceptance that they have hit largely what they were aiming at. Year in and year out, most students have gone off to their colleges with lots of hope, energy, and their heads held high. So shall the current high school students.

But done well, or done poorly, this task in their lives is, indeed, completed. The high school guidance department has submitted student grades to college admissions offices. While getting good grades isn't the only motivation for educational labors, it has been a major engine, particularly of late, as they've had to focus on college applications. Now, for sure, this game's over. The referee has blown the final whistle. The scoreboard is turned off. Yet, students remain, still contending with high school course assignments, tests, and homework, albeit with vastly reduced motivation.

Any other time in a person's working life, once the work-task is accomplished, the bridge built, the law passed, the patient cured, the book published, the tomatoes picked, workers pack their bags, go elsewhere, get on with the next things. But not here. Students have, by law, several months of high school left.

This might have made sense if high school was an ending of academic life before beginning a working life. Society made sure students acquired a determined body of knowledge before they left their childhood community. But for young people in the world today, high school might be seen to exist as a proving ground, a place to sort out where they go next.

In a world more attuned to the actual conditions of contemporary high school students, they would graduate by February 6 or so. They might start college on March 1 or May 1. America elects a president in the beginning of November. They are in office two months later. It might be agreed that this is a larger transition than the one from high school to college.

But colleges have their own rhythm. They say they need the time, from February through August, to decide who is going where. With electronics such as they are, they might now be able to do the sorting much faster, either for students to start shortly after acceptance, or have second-semester senior grades really matter on college applications. It suits them to have this longer period where young people are suspended. Their priorities determine the seven-month duration.

Second-semester seniors also feel the weight of custom upon their lives. Their parents, and theirs, and theirs, on back, went to four full years of high school. Yet, colleges have gotten more competitive in the last several years. This has ratcheted up the demands on high school students. There's been no adjustment in the felt experience of high school as a pressured time to qualify for college.

Despite their exhaustion, students might gain some learning in those last months that could prove valuable. There may be some math or science to acquire, some interesting history book to read, a poem to ponder, some art or play to perform. The Advanced Placement exams coming at the end of the year may provide a college benefit worth preparing for. Students' pride at having done well in school may fuel them through its final moments. But now it is solely their own self-motivation, such that schooling resembles attendance at a book group, or adult-education class, rather than the system of grades and requirements they have accommodated themselves to over these many years.

For example, an AP English teacher might offer some readings and discussions, of *Frankenstein, Beowulf, Romeo and Juliet,* and other works deemed important for any student's education. There may be a few essays to write, and one longer final one, to prepare for college work. But teachers must understand they don't have anywhere near the power in the relationship they had previously, when grades mattered a great deal. If teachers wish to end well the time with students, they must respect the change in the relationship's power dynamics.

It is difficult to acknowledge this ending. Teachers and parents dedicate their lives helping young people prepare for their futures. It is difficult to let go of that relationship. No one likes being told that a relationship of such affection and power is over. This second-semester senior time fills with conflict. Students avoid, evade, stay silent, and don't learn very much. More's the pity, since if everyone understood the phenomenon of senioritis correctly, it might be a quite useful time.

Student behavior in the second semester, often termed senioritis, is an appropriate, even necessary, reaction to the situation students find themselves in. It is not irrational. They are not betraying their goals or principles. Circumstances not of their devising control their behavior.

Many students have spent sixteen- to twenty-hour days to look their best on college applications. They've had to act in un-adolescent, mini-adult ways.

Deferred growing-up now makes it claim. More time for social life, or just watching TV, or sleeping, sleeping, sleeping. "I can't believe what's gotten into my child!" parents exclaim about their second-semester senior. What has gotten into them is that they've worked way too hard too long. They are now allowing other parts of the experience of living to have time and attention.

This re-claiming of other parts of life ought to be explained to one and all as natural, normal, even as something to be celebrated. Students are recovering from an enormous effort of several years' duration. If a teacher were to talk about this openly, it might help in creating more space for students to enjoy this time.

Life rarely suspends its demands in its steady march. Rather, it just keeps coming at people over their lifetime. Passing courses, making a living, pleasing a boss, achieving goals, and so on may seem to be a definition of life itself. A hiatus means a break from all that. Travelers know the pleasures of being unconnected to the cares of the world around them. Similarly, in this time between the end of high school and the start of college, the here-and-now doesn't matter so much. It's an open space, to be filled with, what? Who knows?

There are endless possibilities and opportunities. Cooking classes. Reading a book that wasn't assigned. Watching a favorite movie again and again. Rehearsing with the band in the garage. Painting or writing poems. Spending every moment with a sweetheart. Talking and laughing for hours and hours. "Loaf, and lie on the grass," as Walt Whitman might suggest. It's free time. After all, no one is keeping score.

Many benefits might derive from embracing this glorious time in students' lives. This can be the time when they fully claim their education as their own business, not something done to please others. They can bring to a close the partnership that has prepared them for college. They can assert that it is, after all, their life they are preparing for. Parents may continue to finance it, given, again, the structures and customs of the society students have had no input in shaping. (Germany, for example, finances university education out of taxes.) But parents' role, where they scrutinized effort, homework, the entire academic life, that's over. This hiatus can be the opportunity to help parents let go of this role.

This hiatus might be a necessary time for students to say goodbye, not just to their parents, or the family they were once an everyday part of, or even to their entire community. They are also saying farewell to their childhoods. Young people may say good riddance to childhood's sense of powerlessness or the bewildering complexity of an adult world they have had little ability to understand. But if being a child was at all a fond experience, humans are ambivalent about acknowledging its termination. Even those for whom childhood was an unending nightmare, nevertheless, yearn for the early experiences they didn't have. It is hard to escape the sense of ending. The hiatus can become a space for the grief to weave its way into the fabric of a life, as the poet Denise Levertov might have it.

Other people might seek to make students feel guilty about how students behave now, as if students owe teachers something. While students ought to attend to the high school graduation requirements to avoid the complications from colleges or the culture that complete refusal might entail, they should do so with no guilt, no regrets, and no excuses. They should feel proud of the labors they've performed for years. Teachers may trust that if students can feel the pride in their efforts, they will find the motivation to take care of the necessary business remaining.

This hiatus ought to be infused with the sense for these second-semester seniors that they are young, smart, beautiful. They don't live in a war or a cholera epidemic zone. Much awaits them in the form of human agony and its moral issues. But not now. Now is the time for them to enjoy this sweet in-between time.

Chapter 21

Ambiguity and Human Decisions in History

Readings: *Copenhagen*, a play by Michael Frayn, and an essay about the play by Thomas Powers.

Such a fabulous modern play. Such richness, complexity, meaningful ideas to offer to young people. It speaks to so much of the twentieth century, its agonies and moral issues. The whole senior-year course might be built around it. It is wonderful when it comes around on the curriculum. The essay by Thomas Powers provides a useful contextualization and points of analysis of the play that help students engage more actively with it.

The play itself introduces students to notions of the theater of ideas. There are just three characters, ghosts actually, since their conversations take place long after they're dead. But, as the wife of Niels Bohr reflects about the two other characters, her husband, Niels Bohr, and Werner Heisenberg,

> And from those two heads the future will emerge. Which cities will be destroyed, and which survive. Who will die, and who will live. Which world will go down to obliteration, and which will triumph. (p. 54)

These two men were physicists, who developed in the 1920s the science involved in splitting the atom. From them came the atomic bomb.

The play involves their discussion, as unsettled ghosts, of what happened at a meeting between them in the fall of 1941. Heisenberg was in charge of the German nuclear research program. Bohr, his former mentor, lived in Nazi-occupied Denmark. The tension of the play comes from considering why they met, and what was said. Was Heisenberg wanting to get help from Bohr, in order to succeed in supplying Hitler with an atomic bomb? Did he want to know what Bohr knew about the British and American efforts to use

107

nuclear physics to build a weapon? Or did Heisenberg seek an answer to the question,

> I simply asked you if as a physicist one had the moral right to work on the practical exploitation of atomic energy. (p. 36)

Heisenberg understands the power and responsibility he has.

> That sooner or later governments will have to turn to scientists and ask whether it's worth committing those [huge] resources—whether there's any hope of producing the weapons in time for them to be used . . . . So they will have to come to you and me. We are the ones who will have to advise them whether to go ahead or not. In the end the decision will be in our hands, whether we like it or not. (p. 40)

If that is, indeed, what Heisenberg was asking, then what actually happened in history becomes quite provocative. Bohr helped build the bomb that the Americans dropped on Nagasaki. Heisenberg's German nuclear program never amounted to much.

Did Heisenberg sabotage his own country's program? That's never really determined, either in the play or in history. But the play does suggest it. This allows the audience to ponder the complexities of involvement in evil. As Heisenberg laments at one point,

> When I went to America in 1949 a lot of physicists wouldn't even shake my hand. Hands that had actually built the bomb wouldn't touch mine. (p. 47)

Heisenberg, in Frayn's telling, maintained control of the German nuclear program, and never produced an atomic bomb for Hitler.

The play suggests that what is now regarded as the paragon of evil, "working for the Nazis," might need rethinking. Perhaps human beings, in their goodness or evil, are far more ambiguous. Evil can't easily be subscribed to Heisenberg, since his work never led to the death of anyone, while, as Bohr says, he did his part in the murder of 100,000 Japanese, mostly women and children.

The historical record isn't clear about what these two scientists said to each other. The play suggests the importance of human beings making moral decisions. What they decide to do has enormous implications. Human beings make history, not the other way around. Bohr claims,

> We put man back at the center of the universe . . . . It starts with Einstein. He shows that measurement—measurement, on which the whole possibility of science depends—measurement is not an impersonal event that occurs with impartial universality. It's a human act, carried out from a specific point of view

in time and space, from the one particular viewpoint of a possible observer. Then, . . . we discover that there is no precisely determinable objective universe. That the universe exists only as a series of approximations. Only within the limits determined by our relationship with it. Only through the understanding lodged inside the human head. (pp. 71–72)

Considering this play might be putting a whole lot of carts before the horse with young people. They haven't had much philosophy, let alone particle physics or twentieth-century European history. The play succeeds, however. in making all these ideas, moral dilemmas, even the power of science in the modern world, quite dramatic and thus memorable. Complex intellectual matters become accessible to the imagination. This transforms what might otherwise be distant or unimportant into active engagement for the students. It shows students a path from merely knowing things, to becoming truly educated persons. This play can demonstrate, in the very drama itself, the power of art to inspire a hunger to learn. It can provide a good introduction to the ideas it offers.

Chapter 22

The English Language's First Story, and its Reverberations

Reading: *Beowulf,* a new verse translation with an introduction by Seamus Heaney.

There are real reasons for high school students to read this, even if its main justification seems to be that it heads the customary list of Don't Leave High School Without It. Maybe they aren't all literary reasons. It may be something of a museum piece. It's short. So having second-semester seniors travel with the Thanes to Denmark to kill a monster or two doesn't put anybody out. Some museum pieces are worth the looking at.

It's the first story in English. Students can see how much the vocabulary, and syntax, the very appearance of the words have transformed over the centuries, as they glance from the Old English on the left-hand page, to Heaney's deft translation on the right. Students ought to have some feeling for the linguistic river they swim in. A superhero's prowess comprises this tale of bloody hand-to-hand combat. The storytelling consciousness of English-speaking people begins with this tale of warriors going across the sea to kill a monster. Seemed to work for Beowulf. Maybe that's why English speakers still do this.

There's art here, as Heaney points out well in his introduction. The poem offers a searing commentary on the violence it depicts, the grief it elicits, the views of the leaders of these people.

Pillage and slaughter have emptied the earth of entire peoples. (line 2265)
It was like the misery felt by an old man
Who has lived to see his son's body
swing on the gallows. He begins to keen
and weep for the boy, watching the raven
gloat where he hangs: he can be of no help.
The wisdom of age is useless to him. (lines 2444–49)

111

At Beowulf's funeral, the poem tells not only of grief, but the fear that the passing of a strong leader evokes, for her and her people.

A Geat woman too sang out in grief:
with hair bound up, she unburdened herself
of her worst fears, a wild litany
of nightmare and lament: her nation invaded,
enemies on the rampage, bodies in piles,
slavery and abasement. Heaven swallowed the smoke. (lines 3150–55)

As Beowulf addresses the leader whose people have been ravaged by the monster Grendel's mother who sought revenge for her offspring's killing, he urges the grieving king,

Wise sir, do not grieve. It is always better
to avenge dear ones than to indulge in mourning.
For every one of us, living in this world
means waiting for our end. Let whoever can
win glory before death. When a warrior is gone,
that will be his best and only bulwark. (lines 1384–89)

This same king has words of caution for the triumphant Beowulf:

Do not give way to pride.
For a brief while your strength is in bloom
but it fades quickly; and soon there will follow
illness or the sword to lay you low,
or a sudden fire or surge of water
or jabbing blade or javelin from the air
or repellant age. Your piercing eye
will dim and darken; and death will arrive,
dear warrior, to sweep you away. (lines 1760–68)

These commentaries shape this old poem into a work of art, that still has meaning for contemporary readers, as something more than a museum piece.

English speakers are still very much in the throes of a warrior culture, as any glance at the front page of a newspaper, or a look at the Pentagon's budget, illustrates. To understand the current world, students ought to read this foundation story carefully. Drones, aircraft carriers, submarines, bombs, the Few Good Men, all harken back to the worldview expressed in this poem. If students are intended to control or change any of this way of thinking and relating to others in the contemporary world, this poem must be included in their education.

Chapter 23

From a Bit of Reading, A Big Idea

Readings: Brief selections from *Don Quixote* by Miguel de Cervantes, translated by Samuel Putnam, and indirectly, "The Imitation of Our Lord Don Quixote" by Simon Leys, in *The New York Review of Books,* June 11, 1998.

Students read enough about Don Quixote for them to get some idea of what the novel is about, and for the thoughts from an essay by Simon Leys to make some sense. Students get exposed to the opening scenes of charging at windmills, Quixote's dedication as a knight by prostitutes, the feminist speech by Marcella, his freeing of the slaves, and Quixote's death. They sample the novel's humor and pathos, and Quixote's absurd heroism. All this allows enough familiarity with the work to then offer the crux of Leys' splendid discussion of the varied literary analyses of Quixote.

It didn't work with students to give them Leys' essay directly. It was too dense, too reliant on layers of background literary knowledge even the best-read young people haven't acquired yet. And, as has been mentioned, these are second-semester seniors here. There's less of an opening to fit ideas through. But they'll listen to what Leys has to say about Quixote.

Leys thinks of *classics* as literature we've liked for a long time:

the main concern of the great literary creators was not so much to win the approval of the sophisticated connoisseurs (which, after all, is still a relatively easy trick) as to touch the man in the street, to make him laugh, to make him cry, which is a much more difficult task.

Don Quixote, which is *the* classic *par excellence,* was written for a flatly practical purpose: to amuse the largest possible number of readers, in order to make a lot of money for the author (who needed it badly).

First and foremost, what is read ought to give readers pleasure. Leys believes this is why people keep reading this 400-year-old book.

Leys argues that Quixote isn't mad. He chooses his quest, and can step out of it, and comment on it. Quixote decides to see the windmills as threatening beings. It isn't a compulsion, but a statement of his belief. He succeeds in his quest to become a knight-errant because he performs the deeds such a vocation calls for him to perform. This connects with the assertion Camus' character Dr. Rieux makes at the end of *The Plague*, that *there is more to admire in humanity than despise.* That's Dr. Rieux's way of seeing the world and his place in it. Both he and Quixote make statements of belief.

Leys wants to view Quixote as a product of a Spanish Christianity, where losing can be understood as an expression of the firmness of the believer's faith. He quotes the wealthy American Ted Turner, who commented that Christianity was a "religion of losers."

How very true! What an accurate definition indeed! . . . . That [the epithet *quixotic*] can be used now in an exclusively pejorative sense not only shows that we have ceased to read Cervantes and to understand his character, but more fundamentally it reveals that our culture has drifted away from its spiritual roots.

A personal note:

I used to work for an organization (like the new NYC mayor Bill DeBlasio) called the *Quixote Center*. We worked on issues, in the late 1980's, that seemed hopeless, like opposition to the death penalty, and the U.S. government support of rebels against the government of Nicaragua.

Leys concludes his essay with a claim very much at the center of this course's educational idea.

The successful man adapts himself to the world. The loser persists in trying to adapt the world to himself. Therefore all progress depends on the loser.

Chapter 24

Love and Violence Among the Young

Reading: *Romeo and Juliet* by William Shakespeare.

There isn't as full a job done with *R&J* as with *Hamlet*. The audience's attention at this point in the year diminishes by the day. But this play offers some powerful analytical points for discussion. A consideration of it can deepen, complicate, and connect this old saw of a theater-piece to contemporary readers.

The play allows for a focus on the notion of *tragedy*. More than sadness, the power of a *tragedy* lies in the tension created by the difference between a sense of what could happen and what the characters enact on the stage. "It didn't have to be this way," an audience feel in the pit of their stomachs, as they witness the deaths and destruction. This sense of *tragedy* runs counter to the idea of *fate*, where nothing a human does makes a difference. Characters meet theirs no matter what they try to do to avoid it. This perspective challenges the play's opening lines. The chorus terms the story one of "star-crossed lovers." The stars had nothing to do with it. Rather, a cascade of decisions made by human beings crushed the two young people.

Nothing about Verona was *fair*. A culture of violence possessed the place. American cities, just now emerging from such a contagion, know full well its impact upon the consciousness and behavior of the young. Even Juliet's most beautiful language expressing her passion toward Romeo reflects a world of dismemberment and death. She first sees Romeo and says, "If he be married, My grave is like to be my wedding bed." (Act 1, scene 5, line 135) She's saying goodbye, and offers, "Yet I should kill thee with much cherishing." (2, 2, 183) Even her sweetest, most often quoted expression of love reflects the world of the abattoir:

Give me my Romeo, and when he shall die,
Take him and cut him out in little stars,   ˙
And he will make the face of heaven so fine
That all the world will be in love with night
And pay not worship to the garish sun. (3, 2, 19)

People who gain distance from the death toll in American cities today know that there's nothing *star-crossed* about a culture of violence. It's composed of disparate factors: poverty, poor policing tactics, bad drug policies, even worse gun laws. Americans may not yet have a complete formula to eliminate urban violence, but it is accepted as a human creation. This ought to be a source of hope. It isn't doom or fate, but rather something built, that ought to be malleable to changes in public policy. The misery can be overcome. It too ought to increase sorrow, because the violence has been permitted to go on so long, cause such human agony and loss of life.

These young people, Romeo, Mercutio, Tybalt, Juliet herself, express the privileged views of the young and rich. As Mercutio lies dying, cursing both houses, it might be said to him, "You mean you didn't know that dueling with sharp swords might lead to actual death?" Only after Romeo kills Tybalt does it occur to him that he's in trouble. These precious young ones had been raised in a protected bubble, feeling servants would see to the nasty details of living. Daddy's money and status insulated them from the consequences of their actions.

This really is Juliet's play. Her inner life is on display far more than Romeo's. Juliet's privilege prompts her impatience. She discovers something she really wants in Romeo and cannot wait. She insists that she should have her gratification right now. From her reaction when she's thwarted, she's clearly used to getting her way. Life hasn't engendered much resourcefulness in daddy's little girl. All that occurs to her to do, when she talks with Fr. Lawrence, is threaten to kill herself if she doesn't get what she wants. Her sense of everything coming her way compounds the typical self-absorption of young people. Outside of her gaze at Romeo, all she can see is herself.

Juliet's dad chooses to curse her when she doesn't do what he commands. He certainly doesn't care how she feels, as she begs him to delay the marriage to Paris. It is going to help him get richer. He isn't about to let some girl-child of his get in the way of that.

The Nurse betrays Juliet. She had been her charge's confidant. Juliet seems to feel the Nurse is the one person she might trust in the world. When the Nurse advises her to marry Paris, all the while knowing Juliet's feelings for Romeo, it isn't simply practical advice from a wise adult. The Nurse is acting as the agent of her employer.

In many productions of the play, the lines and the character of Fr. Lawrence get trimmed or eliminated. Yet, he plays quite a central role in the tragedy. He desires to bring together these two warring families by presenting the fait accompli of their marriage. He acts not simply to facilitate their love. He concocts a plan where the two young ones take all the risk. Despite the treacherous nature of communications in that time, he sends only one messenger.

Yet, the inept manipulation of vulnerable young people has little bearing on his most serious failing. There in the tomb, he fears he will be discovered as the mastermind behind all this trouble. He knows Juliet, with her lover and Paris already dead, will probably kill herself. She has threatened suicide before. Romeo's dagger lies right there. Fr. Lawrence runs away. His cowardice means she dies.

And what do the two old geezer-dads do, there at the end, with their lovely children self-poisoned, self-stabbed? Juliet's dad makes reference to her dowry. They then compete to see who will erect the most expensive memorials.

Capulet: O Brother Montague, give me thy hand.
This is my daughter's jointure [dowry], for no more
Can I demand.
Montague: But I can give thee more,
For I will raise her statue in pure gold . . . .
Capulet: As rich shall Romeo's by his lady's lie,
Poor sacrifices of our enmity! (5, 3, 296f]

The creators of this culture of violence, this world of privilege and greed they constructed, can't acknowledge their full culpability. Capulet points to *our enmity* but not to his cursing and condemning his own daughter when she didn't give him what he wanted. Expressing sorrow gets done solely in financial terms.

The play as written shows no doom, no ineluctable march toward death. Each of these characters decides what he or she will do. These choices might have been different, had these individual depictions of human beings been brave, or humble, or truly loving or kind to these young people.

Tragedy thus becomes a way to understand the weave between tears and decisions and actions. Terrible things happen to sweet young lovers because of the world made for them to inhabit. Rage and hope begin when the audience understands it didn't have to be this way, in Verona, or in Washington, D.C.

Chapter 25

Some Poems and Poets for
Stand-Alone Classes

Poems:

"Lines Composed a Few Miles Above Tintern Abbey" by William Wordsworth
"Easter, 1916" and "The Second Coming" by William Butler Yeats
"East Coker" by T. S. Eliot

Poems by Wislawa Szymborska

Throughout the year, some stand-alone classes of poems get scheduled. They're very handy for a class that requires no student preparation, like the class after a holiday or right before one, or at the start of the second semester. Students typically are either too distracted or exhausted to count on the majority of them coming to class prepared to discuss some reading. Students show up, they're given a copy of the poem, and away the class goes into the poem. If class time gets lost for snow days or other vagaries, these stand-alone poetry classes are moved to another slot, to preserve the overall monthly schedule.

There's much pleasure in helping transform a blur of words and images into a clear sense of meaning. By the end, students get a feeling of why some person might bother to write a poem. The classes are most often a guided tour, rather than a participatory event. The poem gets read, then various aspects of it get pointed out. "Hey, look at this, and this, and this . . . Put it all together, it means . . . ." The aim is for students to gain a sense that poetry can speak to them and the concerns of their lives.

These poems allow the relationship of art to history to be drawn even closer. In one way or another, poets wrote to speak to the concerns arising from what was happening to them and their world. This allows for students to make an acquaintance with these historical moments. Links between poems and history emerge.

"LINES COMPOSED A FEW MILES ABOVE TINTERN ABBEY" BY WILLIAM WORDSWORTH

Written at the beginning of the nineteenth century, this poem in particular requires some discussion of England at that time. It wasn't the semi-socialist, mostly tolerant, getting-diverse, largely peaceful parliamentary democracy it now is. (If Americans had lost the Revolutionary War, the country would have gun control, national health insurance, and soccer as the national game. American slavery would have been gone by the 1830s, with no civil war. All of Ireland might have been depopulated, rather than much of it, by 1850, but few would have starved. World War II would have ended in British favor far sooner. But America won its independence, and got to do its own history.)

England at the start of the nineteenth century was Russia today, or maybe Burma or Uruguay: a rigid oligarchy, with a few rich and many poor, and rampant injustice, no constitutional freedoms of the press, assembly, or protest. Their political and social system was maintained with violence by the army and the police. The French Revolution petrified the English oligarchs, as they might now be called, although they preferred to call themselves the nobility. They feared French mayhem and slaughter of the nobility might travel to England. English literary artists who cared about human suffering, like William Wordsworth, faced much danger and difficulty expressing their vision of a more just and equitable society. Wordsworth initially viewed the French Revolution with much hope for his own country, even traveling to France in the Revolution's early months.

The poem begins with a very specific date, July 13, 1798. That would be similar to an American poet listing July 3 or even September 10, as the date of composition. Both those dates would have reference to pivotal events in American history, either the Declaration of Independence, or the terrorist attacks. For the French, their revolution began on July 14, 1789. The date for the poem is one day less than 10 years. In that ensuing time, a bloodbath in France consumed both the nobility and the originators of the revolution, crushing its promise. Artists like Wordsworth fell into despair. The question on his mind, as he wrote, would have been similar to the one facing Albert Camus after WWII. In the face of so much horror, what hope for humanity might there be?

Tintern Abbey, though built originally as a religious institution, had, by the time the poet visited, become a haven for the poor. If a contemporary poet had very carefully noted the location of his poem as near a homeless shelter, this would be a clear indication of its focus on the plight of these suffering people. Wordsworth hints at his focus because of the threat of repression. He couldn't simply ask what hope there could be, when the choices were either France's agony or England's. He'd have been thrown in prison, his books burned. But by making reference to the date and the place, he could orient his poem as he wished it to be read.

In the first section (lines 1–22), he's returning to a place previously visited. The date and place indicate a heavy heart. While it possesses much natural beauty for him, it isn't a wilderness. He describes a place of human habitation, of cottages and orchards and farms, in harmony with the natural world. He indicates, however, as he compares the smoke rising from the cottages to *vagrant dwellers* and *Hermit's cave* that the plight of such people is on his mind.

The second section (lines 23–57) describes how this vision of harmony influences the way he feels and behaves. He feels generous.

—feelings, too
Of unremembered pleasure: such, perhaps,
As have no slight or trivial influence
On that best portion of a good man's life,
His little, nameless, unremembered acts
Of kindness and of love. (lines 30–35)

This vision allows him to see beyond this *unintelligible world*. This *mood* means *we can see into the life of things*. Being in this place, for him, enables him to see a reality that lies beyond his despair. He's relied on this vision many times. *How often has my spirit turned to thee!*

In the third section (lines 58–111), he declares *I dare to hope* because of this vision. It's not the unexamined hope of a young man. *That time is past,* he tells us. He claims that aging has made life better.

Not for this
Faint I, nor mourn nor murmur: other gifts
Have followed; for such loss, I would believe,
Abundant recompense. (lines 85–88)

This vision allows him to hear *the still, sad music of humanity* (line 91), permitting him to feel *a presence that disturbs me with the joy/of elevated thoughts* (lines 93–95). *Something* is in everything. It's everywhere—in *the light of setting suns,* the *ocean,* the *air,* the *blue sky,* and, most significantly, *in the mind of man.* Wordsworth often gets tagged as a nature poet, celebrating the world of nature as apart from humans. This poem shows he's connecting nature and humanity at the very core of his vision.

This is a wonderful poem. Where else in this secular day and age might young people ponder the spiritual world?. It's almost impossible to get students to think about these matters that have been at the center of much of civilization for centuries. The central purpose expressed in art and music, cathedrals and empires, has been an idea of the spirit. Wordsworth asserts the spirit as *the anchor* of his life. It forms his *moral being*.

There's more. In the last section of the poem (lines 112–59), he's actually speaking all the time not to general readers but to his *dear* sister. *Thou art with me here upon the banks/of this fair river.* His affectionate connection with her enables his vision. It's not simply the natural world, existing in harmony with unknown human beings, but the intimacy he shares with his sister that allows him to see what he sees, feel what he feels. The *hope* engendered by this *vision* permits a *cheerful faith* (lines 133–34).

As with Camus' Dr. Rieux, an unprovable assertion counteracts his despair. In the face of the evident horror and human misery of WWII, the doctor claims, *there's more to admire in humanity than despise.* The poet here writes *all which we behold/is full of blessings.* It might, in fact, be quite possible to demonstrate the absurdity of either of these propositions. Yet, there they are. Wordsworth claims *faith* wards off despair. His poem wishes people to understand that guided by love's human connection, meaning and purpose in life can be found. The literary world honors this poem and this poet because of his ability to articulate a way to go on trying, loving, hoping, despite the terrible events of history.

"EASTER, 1916" BY WILLIAM BUTLER YEATS

This poem allows sharing some bits of Irish history, specifically its centuries-long struggle for independence. Earlier in the course, students saw how Seamus Heaney celebrated the eighteenth-century *croppies.* They had been inspired by both the American and French Revolutions to fight for an Ireland free of England. English forces had destroyed them. In the nineteenth century, English policy toward Ireland became a laboratory to perfect methods of colonial occupation and control throughout the world. England established a strong Protestant group of settlers, rewarded them for loyalty to the Crown against the Catholic majority. The potato famine of the mid-nineteenth century became an opportunity to remove millions of Irish farmers from their land, resettled with English or Irish Protestant nobility.

In the early twentieth century, the Great War presented those who struggled for Irish independence an opportunity to collaborate with the Germans against the English. The Germans agreed to supply the Irish rebels with guns and ammunition for a rebellion. When the Germans thought of how the English might retaliate by arming restive groups struggling against German control, they demurred. This left the Irish, already organized for revolt, without the weapons for revolt.

The revolutionary army the rebels had constructed decided to wait for a better time to revolt. But the artists and intellectuals of Dublin, who were the spiritual center of the struggle for Irish freedom, decided they would declare their independence, seize as much of Dublin as they could with the few weapons they possessed. With only a few thousand fighters, poorly armed, they knew it was a suicide mission. They believed their cause needed martyrs and blood to be spilled. This would inspire the Irish people to work for independence.

The English sent over thousands of battle-hardened troops from England. They destroyed a third of Dublin rooting out the rebels. The English held secret military trials, and executed the Irish rebel leaders. Yeats, as a playwright and intellectual in Dublin at the time, knew them all. He, too, cared about independence for his country, but didn't join the rebels.

In the first section of Yeats' poem, he talks of meeting them in the streets, sharing a joke, offering *polite meaningless words*. But yet *all changed*. These people embraced a political, deadly cause. Yeats devises an oxymoron to characterize their change, *a terrible beauty*. Throughout the poem, he develops his sense of this ambivalence, of something wonderful in their actions, yet also full of dread.

In the second section, he enumerates several specific people he knew well who had *resigned his part/in the casual comedy*. Some he liked, others he didn't. They were different now.

> At this point I pause and look around the room at my students. Some may join the military or the police in a year or two. Others may risk their lives in foreign countries working for a refugee organization. "You, too, might find that the sweet, happy life you're envisioning for yourselves gets put aside, as you respond to some voice, some cause, calling to you, or to your friend. It's this sense our poet wishes us to experience. There's sadness as someone is *transformed utterly*. There may be mystery, awe, maybe even some fear about what human beings are capable of in their lives. All this lies ahead of you, our poet suggests."

His third section articulates some of the *terrible* side of his ambivalence. His friends have dedicated themselves to death, either their own, or of those who will oppose their struggle for Irish freedom. They *trouble the living stream,* these people with *hearts with one purpose alone*. Everybody and everything else exists in time, which *minute by minute they change*. Only this *stone* doesn't. It seems an image that expresses both power and fear for the poet. *The stone* persists, enchanting *hearts.*

   Particularly, he notes, starting off the final section, that

Too long a sacrifice
Can make a stone of the heart.

   We understand he's in the middle of a great struggle inside himself. He's trying to focus on memorializing their sacrifice, but he keeps asking *when will it suffice?* Let *Heaven* deal with this, he responds the first time. He does circle back to the question, as he asks, *was it needless death after all?* He wishes to have the English answer that question. But he asks a third time,

And what if excess of love
Bewildered them till they died?

   He has no answer. He just wishes to celebrate them, even if what this *beauty* has evoked is *terrible.*

   If the stirring words of the very people he names in the poem get brought into the discussion, students might understand how powerful this sacrifice was to the Irish who wished freedom for their country.

   This is Pearse at his court-martial:

When I was a child of ten I went down on my bare knees by my bedside one night and promised God that I should devote my life to an effort to free my country. I have kept that promise. As a boy and as a man I have worked for Irish freedom, first among all earthly things. I have helped to organize, to arm, to train, and to discipline my fellow countrymen to the sole end that, when the time came, they might fight for Irish freedom. The time, as it seemed to me, did come, and we went into the fight. I am glad we did. We seem to have lost. We have not lost. To refuse to fight would have been to lose; to fight is to win. We have kept faith with the past, and handed on a tradition to the future.

   I assume that I am speaking to Englishmen, who value their freedom and who profess to be fighting for the freedom of Belgium and Serbia. Believe that we, too, love freedom and desire it. To us it is more desirable than anything in the world. If you strike us down now, we shall rise again and renew the fight. You cannot conquer Ireland. You cannot extinguish the Irish passion for freedom. If our deed has not been sufficient to win freedom, then our children will win it by a better deed.[1]

MacDonagh:

You [English soldiers] will be proud to die for Britain, your Imperial patron, and I am proud and happy to die for Ireland, my glorious Fatherland . . . The

Proclamation of the Irish Republic [their Declaration of Independence] has been adduced in evidence against me as one of the signatories; you think it already a dead, a buried letter, but it lives, it lives. From minds alight with Ireland's vivid intellect, it sprang; in hearts aflame with Ireland's mighty love, it was conceived. Such documents do not die.[2]

Connolly:

Katherine Tynan, the poetess, has left a description of Connolly's
death as it was related to her by Surgeon Richard Tobin who
had been called in to attend to the wounded rebel.
"Can I do anything for you, Connolly?"
"I want nothing but liberty."
"You must go to the Shan Van Vocht [knickname for Ireland]
for that. Can I do anything to make you easier?"
"What do you think will happen to me?" asked Connolly.
"You'll be shot."
"Oh, you think that?"
"I am sure of it."
"Why?"
"They can't do anything else. Can they buy you?"
"No."
"Can they frighten you?"
"No."
"Will you promise if they let you off with your life to
go away and be a good boy for the future?"
"No."
"They can do nothing else but shoot you."
"Oh, I recognize that," said Connolly."[3]

Despite Yeat's ambivalence, he wished to honor the dedication and sacrifice of these people in this poem. How he might further address his ambivalence will be seen in other poems.

"THE SECOND COMING" BY WILLIAM BUTLER YEATS

This poem, written five years later, serves to engage further with the questions he raised in "Easter, 1916." By that time, The Great War had ended in misery and defeat for both Germany and Russia, with the growth of violent new ideologies in both countries. The death of his Irish revolutionaries, while it did serve to inspire a successful guerilla campaign that led to the Irish Free State, didn't seem so clearly heroic as it had initially. Or perhaps he understood that even heroism itself presents a troubling idea. What Yeats felt was stirring wasn't a sense of cooperation for a better world, but rather a rise of fanaticism in these war-ravaged countries. It would soon be termed Nazism and Communism. Both have their origins in the aftermath of the war. What he had once celebrated, at least in part, as sacrifice of life for a cause, he now believes severs the connection among human beings.

The first section of "The Second Coming" describes a vision of a terrible world of disintegration and death. Everything is coming *apart*. What had been central to humans' relations with one another can't hold people together anymore. Slaughter pervades, innocence is crushed. Good people aren't strong in their beliefs. Evil gathers much power to itself.

Maybe all this chaos means the end of the world is coming. That's what "Second Coming" involves, in the Christian idea that Christ would return then. Yeats suggests a more ominous arrival, out of this spirit of the age (the *Spiritus Mundi*). Some force, some figure, that has abided in humanity for almost its entire historical existence now comes alive. Will this save the world? He asks, mockingly. He knows it won't.

With the advantage of almost a hundred years, the world knows how absolutely correct Yeats' foreboding vision was. He's telling readers that the murder of human beings, by bombs, bullets, starvation, disease, that many had thought was all behind humanity is only now getting started, at the conclusion of this war-to-end-wars. From the fanaticism he felt existed in the Irish rebels, he looks toward much larger countries, with millions of people beginning to be shaped into powerful military foes. By mid-century, this *rough beast* will have, indeed, devoured countless millions.

It's all there, in his poem, in his vision that countered the hopes of many that communism would bring forth the New Man, or that fascism would mold the Master Race. He saw the horror that stone-hearts might unleash, for their Causes. He wants human beings to value human life, its history, the ways devised to honor what people do with their lives. He asks, in another closely related poem, "Prayer for my Daughter":

How but in custom and in ceremony
Are beauty and innocence born?

Yeats thus stands as a powerful voice against the certainties of the totalitarian revolutionaries, of either the left or the right. Human civilization, in its complex richness, ought not to be done away with because of an idea of something better. The contemporary world seems to have embraced his caution, and discredited the fanatics. As people regard their own futures, they ought to incorporate his caution and sensitivity to *beauty and innocence*.

"EAST COKER" BY T. S. ELIOT

This poem is so rich, so complex, it would need far more time in class than can be allowed in a one-class-per-poem format. Students get some points of observation, which might help them begin to think about the poem, or perhaps think along with it. Throughout the poem, Eliot offers a series of paradoxes to get at deeper truths than might be arrived at by logical thinking. He desires readers to contemplate the unity of opposites. He starts off with the assertion, *In my beginning is my end.* This might evoke some sense of the circularity of history. Rather than regarding humanity as on a march of progress, Eliot invites a regard for human life as part of a circle, of beginnings and endings that converge.

In his first stanza, he invokes the language of the Biblical book, Ecclesiastes:

To every thing there is a season, and a time to every purpose under heaven:
A time to be born, and a time to die; a time to plant, and a time
to pluck up that which is planted;. Ecclesiastes, 3, 1

This serves to connect him with language from the distant past that offered the same notion.

In the middle of his second section, he steps back from what he's telling us, to comment on it, how it might be coming across to us. He cuts down his own presentation, terming it *a periphrastic study in a worn-out poetical fashion.* He becomes his own opposite, a critic of his own poem. This permits him to go deeper, speak more bluntly to readers.

He then offers some thoughts that might be particularly liberating to young students. He declares:

There is, it seems to us,
At best, only a limited value
In the knowledge derived from experience.
The knowledge imposes a pattern, and falsifies,
For the pattern is new in every moment
And every moment is a new and shocking
Valuation of all we have been.

Students really like reading that. Many adults hold their greater level of experience in living over them as a method of control. To have this poet assert that there's not really much good in that experience allows students a greater sense of confidence. They can devise their own way of living and of seeing the world. Especially when that sense gets combined with Eliot's coupling of *wisdom* with *humility,* young people feel a sense of empowerment in thinking about this poem.

In the third section, Eliot, like Camus' Dr. Rieux, and William Word-sworth, invites his readers to consider the paradoxical nature of *faith*. The proof of a God, or of the goodness of humanity, might not seem to be available, yet the doctor, after the horror of WWII, or the poet, after the French Revolution's terror, asserts his *faith*. Even Zora Neale Hurston, in her novel *Their Eyes Were Watching God*, suggests the unity of the opposites, as Eliot does:

let the dark come upon you
Which shall be the darkness of God.

Wait, Eliot proclaims to readers, without *hope*, without *love*, without *thought*. As Hurston herself might have said, *So the darkness shall be the light, and the stillness the dancing*. This, of course, makes no sense to them. It need not. But its non-sense might find its way into their memory, and their reflections on their lives. Such might be the process to insight.

At the end of the third section, Eliot gets at the central paradox of learning, growing, gaining insight and maturity. Such a journey involves *no ecstasy*, it is *the way of ignorance, of dispossession*. Further,

And what you do not know is the only thing you know
And what you own is what you do not own
And where you are is where you are not.

All these riddles might create a whiplash. With a light touch, however, this poem might create some opportunities to make a deeper sense of their process of growing up.

Section four offers the notion of *the wounded surgeon*. This combination of opposites permits entry into *compassion*. Doctors, social workers, therapists, helpers of any kind, who have lost touch with their own woundedness can't be very useful at the *healer's art*, Eliot suggests. Only when these opposites combine can such a person be useful to someone else.

Being a Christian, Eliot extends his paradoxes to include the one that forms the central part of the Christian faith. God sacrificed himself, Christians believe, for the benefit of humanity. *In spite* of the terrible death of the Christian Savior, Eliot observes, *we call this Friday* [the day Jesus was crucified] *good*.

In section five, the poet gets to the central paradox of writing. His time has been *largely wasted*. It might serve as much consolation for young people to understand that this renowned poet feels his life's work has been *wasted*. Eliot connects his feeling with the historical moment, anchoring his thoughts in the time between WWI and WWII (*l'entre deux guerres—between two wars*). The world was quite going to hell at that time. Any effort he might expend as a poet, even as a human being, was of no use. His helplessness was total. Such feelings seem to come with the writing trade. Even if writers say something that's real, that says what they want it to say, it *has already been discovered once or twice, or several times.* What should writers do?

For us, there is only the trying.
The rest is not our business.

Humans live in a world, he's telling us, filled with paradox. All they can do is keep working to understand, and talk to other people about this.

What should humanity strive for? *A further union, a deeper communion.* It is the connection of one to the other, in the face of a world of riddles, of opposites that can't be understood, that must be the aim. It is the *love* for each other that *is most nearly itself/When here and now cease to matter.* Exactly what that means will have to be worked out by each person in living his or her life.

That's a whole lot for eighteen year olds to get their minds around. Even for someone who has been reading the poem for fifty years, and spent time as a Zen Buddhist working on far simpler riddles, the pondering this poem offers goes beyond one lifetime. But it seems worthwhile to introduce such a presentation of nonlogical thinking that poetry can provide to young people, even if the understanding of it might be gained many years in the future.

POEMS OF WISLAWA SZYMBORSKA

The course ends with the poems of a compatriot of Czeslaw Milosz, a Polish poet from the post-WWII generation. After many classes, much talk, the finish is with her words. The poems are read in class. Students have their say. The class is over. The full poems can be found in her volume, *View with a Grain of Sand.*

Her poem "Tortures" has some tragic relevance in our time. It begins by asserting "Nothing has changed" by which she means that torture, as a human practice, is thousands of years old. While "the manners, ceremonies, dances" have changed, humanity still suffers from the pain caused by others. "The body is and is and is," she concludes. A sobering reminder, given Abu Ghraib and black sites.

In "The Century's Decline," Szymborska reflects on how "Our Twentieth Century was going to improve on the others." It has not, she understands. The sad history of this time reveals how much misery and evil humanity has unleashed. "How should we live?" she quotes a friend asking. Still the most important question for young people to answer.

In "Reality Demands" the poet asserts that, despite everything, "life goes on." She recites the names of famous, destroyed places, from Jericho to Hiroshima. Humanity has rebuilt them, gone on. Alongside the tragedy of history, then, lies the irrepressible vitality of humanity.

A good note, to end this course on.

NOTES

1. Quoted in *1916: The Easter Rising* by Tim Pat Coogan, p. 164.
2. Quoted in *Michael Collins and the Troubles, The Struggle for Irish Freedom, 1912–1922,* by Tim Pat Coogan, p. 101.
3. Ibid., p. 102.

Chapter 26

How to Deal with Pushy Parents

Here are some thoughts about how to cope with those nagging, pesky, irritable people that keep getting in the face of teachers, at classroom conferences, via emails, phone calls, before school, after school, even at the supermarket on Saturday. Following this advice ought to make it much easier for teachers to contend with pushy parents.

All good parents are pushy. It's their job. The ones who aren't, who see their offspring as servants, wish-fulfillers, or life-companions, or don't care much about their children's fate, present far more problems for the development of the young and the fate of society. The world depends upon parents who advocate and defend, who push aggressively, subtly, persistently, for what they perceive as their children's best interest.

Parents, students, and teachers, organized for the purpose of preparing the young for their future, ought to form a powerful coalition. A parent in conflict with a teacher indicates this natural order out of kilter. A unified commitment toward the educational goal should be the coalition's focus.

As with any coalition, conflict may occur among its participants. Parents' individual view of educational issues differs from that of a teacher, who is contending with multitudes of students. Administrators are often too busy to offer meaningful supervision to teachers. Principals, even department chairs, usually possess a bureaucratic perspective that differs from what matters to the individual student. Students themselves are typically too vulnerable or not articulate enough to contend with the powerful adult teacher to advocate effectively on their own behalf. Although sometimes blunt and unsympathetic, parents often give voice to critical concerns of the specific educational practice in the classroom. Parents offer teachers valuable supervision.

Only parents can inquire about the fairness of specific grades, or how their child was treated in a class discussion, or the educational purpose of daily classroom work. But teachers too ought to want grading policies to be clearly understood and just, to establish a tolerant classroom environment, and have students understand how their labors will contribute to their academic future. There's no division between a teacher and parents about these goals.

There may occasionally be gangster-parents ("Either there's an A, or your brains, on my child's report card") who petition for special treatment, regardless of fairness or their child's effort. They can be dealt with, either by granting the A, or by employing heroic measures, depending on the teacher's proclivities. But most parents want the same genuine education for the students that the teacher wants. If teachers view complaints from parents in this framework, they may understand what needs to be done, or undone, or apologized for and adjusted, in their classroom practice.

Maybe in college classes, grading can be based on a student's brilliance. But high school classes ought to embody the notion that if the student performs the assigned work with due diligence, then a good grade can be achieved. That's a principle that all three members of the coalition can usually agree on. There may be part of everyone, at least among the adults in the coalition, that understands the work goes much easier when there's considerable interest in the material. But the coalition can work well if everyone agrees that doing the assignments, reading the books, paying attention in class, taking notes result in a good grade. Evaluation then becomes quite simply a matter of whether the student did the work or not.

Even when the grading policies are clear, the classroom is tolerant, and the educational purpose and its pursuit by diligent labor are shared by parents and the teacher, the student may actually not perform very well. Like youth coaches, pediatricians, and children's theater directors, teachers might have an evaluation of the student at variance with the parents' own idea of their offspring. The language any evaluator of young people uses must reflect the fraught nature of their task as bearers of bad tidings. Such messengers need to accept they are vessels for the rage or grief that such an unhappy view might evoke. It's part of the teaching job, an element of the coalition's necessary work.

In particular, younger teachers, not yet schooled by their own offspring in the vicissitudes of parenting, must keep in mind that it will never do to blame parents for a lousy job of child-raising. A good doctor wouldn't focus on the bad parenting of an overweight child. A good coach or director wouldn't find fault with parents for not preparing their child to perform. Even if a teacher's own humility doesn't inform his or her discourse, the only possible language for a teacher should be based on consolation and encouragement for the future.

A teacher might also trust that beneath whatever blustery mask the parents might maintain, they possess sufficient guilt and awareness of their flaws as parents. For young students not doing well in school, already burdened by how much of a disappointment they are to their parents, the best that a teacher might do would be to point to future effort to rectify an unpromising present. Hope might dissolve despair. A teacher's efforts with both ought to be centered on freeing up the young students from the adults' expectations, so that they might discover their own.

If teachers lack compassion for those young people afflicted with more than the typical turbulence of adolescence, it would be best, for the sake of the coalition, if the teachers kept such a shortfall to themselves. American society and its psychotherapeutic professions acknowledge that mental illness does exist. It inhibits or prevents intellectual concentration. A depressed teenager can no more read a book than a person with a broken leg can play soccer.

It ought to be sufficient evidence for the teacher if the parents, or the students, claim they are afflicted. There may be a few manipulative coalition members out there, but, like gangster-parents, they are a rarity. What the teacher gains in coalition-building with their acceptance and trust in the self-reporting is well worth the risk that some cynic would be bluffing to get out of the work. Teachers whose classroom policies regard mental illness as they would a bout of serious physical illness will allow students to contend with this incapacitation and the demands of academic life as best as they are able.

In the coalition, the teacher possesses the most freedom to act to ensure its effective functioning. Parents, despite their desires, hardly have much immediate sway with their teenage children. So much of student performance is determined by the vast river of society, of its zip codes' visions and strictures, early childhood vocabulary, DNA and its unfolding. Students may bring hunger that overcomes limitations, yet they are hardly in complete control of their fate. It will take maturity for them to genuinely carve out their own place in the world. Detached from the anguish inherent in getting an education, the teacher has the most ability in the coalition to adjust and change.

Teachers need to demonstrate their professionalism. They can strive to make sure grades are clearly and fairly arrived at; they can protect individual students who express unpopular views during classroom discussions; they can articulate the link between the daily tasks and the academic future. Teachers can develop language appropriate to difficult situations. They can learn to say, "I'm so sorry," to grieving parents, and "Keep at it, you'll have lots of chances to build a life," to despairing young people.

The best way to deal with pushy parents thus becomes a matter of listening to them and adjusting accordingly.

Chapter 27

Teaching as Both a Possible and an Impossible Job

INTRODUCTION

This is a huge topic. It would take another book to explore the themes fully. What follows ought then to be read as something of a position paper, a touching upon an argument for differentiating between possible and impossible jobs in teaching.

It starts with the premise: It is very hard to teach human beings anything of value.

There's so much that restricts a teacher influencing the way students see themselves or the world. They don't enter the classroom as bright-eyed, eager clean slates, ready to have knowledge poured into them. Their outlook, attitude, and previous life experiences largely determine what can happen in the classroom. All thinkers who have followed upon Freud and Marx in psychology and sociology have delineated how consciousness forms before or outside of formal education. It is difficult for a person to be open to a life-altering idea, or even one that shifts his or her perspective.

Lawrence Tribe, one of America's preeminent liberal law school professors, had Supreme Court Chief Justice John Roberts as his student. Roberts' rulings have been uniformly conservative. A lesson in humility for all teachers. Despite a teacher's best efforts, students may go on seeing the world the way they always have.

That's why this book has tried to point out carefully how a teacher might be most effective. Even under the most propitious of circumstances, the human mind and psyche work against good teaching.

CONSENT

Imagine two groups, both constituted for a cause. One is a group of volunteer forest fire fighters. The other is what was once called a press-gang, formed of men abducted from eighteenth-century British roads and villages, gathered to fight in the crown's navy. With the firefighters, there's a clear unity of purpose, a vision of the future with the fire extinguished. While the work might be dangerous and arduous, there's group cohesion, as all members have freely chosen to participate. Their leader may give them an order they don't fully understand, but they are willing to comply because they trust the goals, the effort, the leadership.

Contrast that with the press-gang. There's considerable resistance, resentment, and even subversion of the group's goal. Only force compels minimum compliance. Members focus much anger on the person attempting to direct their activities. Constant tension exists between members and leader. The only vision of the future for the group members involves escape from the strenuous duties imposed.

The firefighters exhaust themselves fighting the fire. At the end of the day, at the end of the season, they're glad to take a break, but satisfied with the meaning and effectiveness of their work. The other group, filled to the brim with the resentments and conflicts that lie at the heart of the enterprise, yearns only for freedom. As soon as possible, their leader seeks other employment.

The difference between possible and impossible teaching positions becomes a matter of whether the group eventually consents to the task. While every teacher must transform what is, at least in structure, a press-gang, into a group willing to work toward a goal, many factors outside the teacher's control determine whether such a transformation can occur.

THE APPLE

This book embodies the belief that the work of a teacher can be full of satisfaction and meaning, forever interesting, absorbing, and engaging, because of its ability to influence students' lives. Once educators understand what is possible, they may develop a practice of sustainable, even pleasurable, employment.

But context may render teaching an impossible job. The circumstances the teachers find themselves in can drive them crazy, or, even worse, to cynicism, despair, and thus Wall Street. Upton Sinclair, an early-twentieth-century reformer, declared that the source of human suffering wasn't Adam or Eve, or even the snake. It was "the apple," that is, the structure of the economic and political world. Similarly, the difference between a possible and an impossible teaching job involves the nature of the apple, the structure of the school itself.

If "the apple" consists of a coalition of students, their parents and the teacher working together to provide an education for the young people, then much may be possible in the classroom. Students show up, and are ready and willing to learn. They do their homework and class assignments. When problems arise, the coalition meets to work them out. Students demonstrate by their behavior that they understand schooling exists to prepare them for their futures. They come into the classroom, even in first grade, already connecting a life of the mind with classroom activities, bringing to bear their imagination and curiosity to their school lives. Stories and other art forms feed their souls. There's a respectful autonomy and collaboration of school administration over matters of curriculum and pedagogy. To work with such a constituted group becomes a labor of love.

It's not possible for a person to teach if these factors aren't present to a significant degree. If parents are inattentive or indifferent, if administrators prescribe or proscribe curriculum and pedagogy, then teachers will have a much harder time in the classroom. But the most important factor in an effective educational coalition involves the attitude or consciousness of the students themselves. If students avoid school or don't do homework or class assignments, if they view the teacher as the enemy or the oppressor, then teaching can't really happen. The work of education gets thwarted if students haven't developed a life of the mind that gets engaged with schoolwork, if imagination, creativity, and stories exist only outside the classroom, and not inside it.

In America today, the ravages of racism and poverty impede young people from developing an academic vision for their lives. Insecure housing, inadequate health care, and fraught human relationships intrude upon the concentration of students. Anger and fear inhibit the mind's focus on the particulars of schooling. Precious little teaching can happen in a room with twenty or thirty or more such afflicted young people. It is a cruel fantasy for teaching recruitment programs to enlist recent college graduates to work in such impossible school environments. Of course, these young teachers leave after a couple of years of frustration and agony. The job is impossible.

In most schools, there's a mix of both types of students. Most young people are just going through high school, wanting to get done with this thing, so their lives can begin. There's even a blend of both inside the psyche of each young person. Left to their own devices, almost none would go to school, or get that involved in the labor of learning. They might let the forest burn, if they were having fun.

THE DIFFERENCE

The issue is proportionality. When a large part of the student body, and each student's psyche, goes along with the educational endeavor then that cooperation can enfold the natural reluctance to work that all humans possess, particularly former children. Students engage with school since they agree with its goals, anticipate taking their place in this society in the future, even find pleasure in developing their minds and meeting the challenges of learning. The teacher can be seen as an ally, even if this leader is pushing students to work harder than they might without such a figure in their group.

Young people ambivalent about their consent to schooling benefit from associating with students who are much more committed. They witness what's possible. That's why it would be dreadful to exclude, as "school-choice" advocates would have it, those who haven't yet gotten involved in their own learning. Schools ought to be inclusive of all young people on this spectrum.

Yet, if teachers find themselves contending with a vast majority of students who don't want to be there in school, who don't see how its activities pertain to them or their futures, who find that it doesn't connect to their interests, or imaginations, or it isn't satisfying to them to labor and learn what schools offer, then it will be hell to teach in such a school.

The hero myth makes it worse. Hollywood loves to crank out that notion of the teacher as savior, or saint, or superman. The myth of the super-teacher involves this person transforming a group of hostile conscripts into eager students in a few months. Only the young teacher for a year or two can bear the burden of such a fantasy. "Burn-out" as it's termed, comes from trying to fulfill the myth. More experienced teachers don't get "burned-out" because they know to avoid slogans and being blamed for what they can't control. They understand it is nonsense to believe this myth of the heroic individual teacher, by dint of will and strong belief, overcoming the resistance of the press-gang. Slogans blind the sloganeer to the reality of what is happening.

Myth-makers assert that the heroic teacher can motivate young people to do schoolwork. "Let's go fight this fire," works if those assembled consent to this work, fully understanding its purpose. Not so much with those kidnapped and coerced to fight. Myth-makers deny the power of the culture formed by those who have been alienated for generations from the majority culture. Young people raised and nurtured in such a separate world regard education as forcing them to choose between their people and a strange foreign world.

Such students' consciousness may be ill-conceived, misinformed, and immature. Nevertheless, these are the real attitudes of human beings. They may be malleable over time, but people rarely change these fundamental aspects of themselves quickly, particularly at the behest of someone they initially regard as forcing them to do something.

Certainly all children can learn. But that's not the point. What matters is whether they access their desire to acquire an education. To learn anything of value requires constant and difficult labor. Minds of human beings are remarkably the same. It is the hearts that vary greatly.

THE SEPARATION

The task for a teacher involves separating the genuine possibilities of education from the myth that anything is possible. The process involves understanding the difference between idealism and fantasy. "School reformers" who espouse slogans and myth, and make policy on that basis, make the job of teaching impossible in those contexts where it is at best quite difficult.

There are many teachers who have made do with jobs that might seem impossible. They view their task as social work, or transformation, or simply expressing kindness to young people, caught in painful or hopeless situations. These are honorable, even noble undertakings. Much might be accomplished by assisting students struggling to come of age in difficult circumstances. The comfort and support of a caring adult can make all the difference in a young person's life. Some young people might also be changed by a persistent, faithful teacher insisting on the benefits of an education. But these tasks are separate from the actual teaching of students.

There might also be the possibility of restructuring the classroom to address the issue of students' lack of consent to their education. Counseling, mentoring, small group work, and creative approaches to the curriculum may yield more cooperation from students, and a sense of their partnership with the teachers. Such modifications of the educational experience would involve the participation of the administration, even the school board, and cost a lot more with the addition of other professionals. If many resources and imagination get focused on eliciting students' active engagement, other worlds may open up for those most alienated from the educational process.

But what must be acknowledged, however, is that maintaining a typical classroom structure, of 25 to 35 or more students who will take every opportunity to express that they really don't believe in the process, or wish to be there, with one teacher contending with 100 or 150 such people every day, well, that will leave the teacher feeling exhausted, frustrated, and hopeless.

THE URGENCY

Teachers and their students today exist in a far different economic context. Large numbers of young Americans for generations used to be able to goof their way through high school, then mature into a job that provided enough for them to support a family. There was no need for a total population to be educated, even all that literate. Much of the economy desired workers who might obediently perform drudging labor.

Now the consequences are dire for the unskilled and unacademic. There's precious little work, and most of it involves what men have traditionally regarded as women's work that excludes or inhibits them. All of the current young generation faces the challenge of genuine education in high school, as preparation for work with a strong component of intellectual activity.

American education needs to 90 quite a distance from the time when it was a crime to teach people of color to read.

Education now finds itself embroiled in the political and social struggles of the times. But the task of teaching students in a school setting is only possible if the students say, with their parents' backing, "Teach me."

Chapter 28

Dealing with Terrible Events

Despite the best efforts of parents and educators to shield the young, some-times the pain of the world intrudes upon the concentration available in a classroom. Something happens out there, and it's on the minds of everyone in the room. With cell phone technology such as it is, there's no way to pre-vent students from immediate access to alarming or tragic news. The buzz, the chatter, and deeper, the anxiety or disturbance, bring any classroom focus to a halt. Nothing cognitive can happen with powerful feelings troubling all students.

What can be done in a classroom the day after terrorists seize commercial airliners and crash them into tall buildings and the Pentagon? If one student from the school kills two fellow students in a jealous rage? If a student in the classroom gets sick and dies? Sometimes joyous events, a sports team's victory, a prom, an African-American being elected president, might be on everyone's mind, that may need attending to. But usually, it is the terrible, sudden events that predominate in interfering with students' concentration. They bring to the fore the evil and death in the world.

Better to stop the class, and discuss what's on everyone's mind. Surrender-ing to the moment presents more educational opportunities than pretending everyone can concentrate. There may be a time and place for a teacher to assume command and state, "Let's get on with it," but that gambit can take place only many days later. If the feelings are large and unexpressed, if the room is full of thoughts about some occurrence, allow all this power to fill the space. It is already doing so, after all. Education is best when it is real.

But how to do this?

There's a device that achieves many worthy objectives. Have students take out a sheet of paper, and anonymously write down their thoughts and feelings about what has happened. Explain to students that the teacher will collect them, then read out loud these thoughts and feelings to the class, with no attribution. Assure students that if they feel too shy to have their thoughts read aloud, the teacher will honor a request to not read it to the class. Have them note this at the top of the page.

Collect their writings, then read them to the class. The teacher may pause after each reading, and make a brief comment, but maybe not. What's mainly important is the students' pondering, the writing, the expressing, and the listening. A teacher's reactions aren't central to the process.

Particularly if the teacher senses that views expressed might be divisive, students ought to be instructed to sit and listen, without registering either approval or disapproval. In the heat of the moment, students may need to be reminded that their task is to respectfully receive the reading of what other students think and feel.

This writing-then-reading exercise will accomplish several worthy goals. All students in the class will have a chance to consider what they think and feel, separate from everyone else, without being influenced in the moment by knowing what others might say. What they write can be more deliberately considered than what they might express verbally. With the anonymous readings, students can listen to the thoughts and feelings without having to associate these utterances with any individual. Students will gain a more collective sense of what thoughts and feelings exist in the room.

They will get practice struggling to find words for what they deeply think and powerfully feel, perhaps the best writing exercise possible. (But be careful not to call it that, lest the teacher be thought to be manipulating a terrible event into a school lesson.)

While there's sometimes more that needs to be said verbally by the students in a class discussion after the reading, typically the process clears the air. If there's class time left, some of what was planned for that day might happen. If a teacher has a hard time letting go of the day's lesson, think of the missed class as a snow day, or any sort of unscheduled interruption. Permit the messiness of life to have its time. Teachers don't really have any choice anyway.

The expressions allow the teacher to find out what sense or non-sense the students make of the disturbing event. The teacher may thus have the opportunity to calm exaggerated fears, to correct or redirect misinformation. But the main effort becomes demonstrating how a painful, frightening event can be coped with in a group setting. Anger, fear, grief, dread, confusion, or other strong feelings, can become part of the group's experience. Such a writing-then-reading activity allows for students to hear their own thoughts read back to them, in a situation that mimics publication. This in itself can be quite instructive.

The teacher ought not to offer much by way of advice, particularly with expressions of feelings. Simply allowing these utterances to be heard by others, without censure, offers a powerful lesson. The teacher may need to instruct students to share in this tolerance, if an unpopular view is expressed. "The United States had it coming to them, after all the terrible things they have done in the world," one student might express, after 9/11. Not a popular view in an American classroom at the time.

If a teacher were to allow that view to be out there, without catcalls or criticisms, this might signal a huge increase in classroom tolerance, and an understanding by everyone in the room that other people may not share one outlook. Such awareness might be deemed crucial for a liberal education. Or the opposite expression, a student saying after 9/11 that he or she hated all Muslims, ought to be accepted as part of what might be felt by people at many moments in history. Certainly that's what Americans felt toward the Japanese after Pearl Harbor was attacked. It's what the Irish have felt for generations toward the British, what Muslims feel toward Hindus, Shiites toward Sunnis, what Bigger Thomas felt toward white people.

The teacher's role ought to be to provide a safe space for the expression of feeling. There's no need to "do" much with such feelings. Allow them to be out in the open. Trust that this in itself is a valuable endeavor.

Teachers may themselves have to fake it. They may be as upset as students. In the classroom setting, this would not be the time to share this with young people. Even if teachers have to pretend, they ought to assume the role of the grownup. The teacher ushers students into the world, with its evil, its horror, its sudden death. For millennia the old have played the role of such a welcoming committee.

Chapter 29

Classroom Management and its Ills

The notion of a teacher creating a classroom environment of understanding, respect, and tolerance for students weaves its way throughout this book. This approach to teaching suggests a belief in the fundamental decency of human beings. If students are treated well, they will cooperate with an education project that they ought to perceive as being in their best interest. They will learn and prepare for their futures, as they understand preparation and future. Students and teachers should unite with a common goal. Cooperation and consent should become the critical concerns, not coercion and compliance.

But a few aspects of the process come into sharp relief if classroom management becomes the lens through which teaching is viewed. Other chapters in this book, like chapter 27 that discusses possible and impossible teaching jobs, have already touched on one element of it. But it may be useful here to focus on classroom management by itself for many reasons. If a teacher has to spend much time and energy contending with student disruptions or if the teacher feels opposed to students, rather than allied, then considering what can be done might help get the educational process back on track.

This can be difficult, even painful. Misbehaving students evoke anger in teachers. They make the teacher feel inadequate. But posing diagnostic questions, despite the discomfort, may suggest what ought to be done to contend with classroom management concerns.

What are the teacher's expectations for the class?

The issue isn't whether a teacher has "high expectations" for students. That phrase implies students have the intelligence to learn. Of course they do. The issue isn't student intelligence, but rather whether their vision of the value of the education differs from the teacher's.

If the teacher has expectations of the pace or content of learning that students can't or won't meet, then what happens in such a class could be considered as resistance to the teacher's imposition. If the teacher's offering makes students feel inadequate, or if students don't understand its importance or relevance for their education, then the students might choose disruption as preferable to submissive misery. A teacher whose daily experience consists largely of frustration and anger usually doesn't understand what students can or will do, and what they won't.

Eager students are usually the ones who become teachers. Yet, those who sat in the front of the class during their student years, engaged in the learning process, end up having a far different experience of school than those who sat in the back of the classroom. These teachers have few points of reference with those students who hated school, for whom the whole thing was a routine torture.

This is why programs that recruit students from elite universities, perhaps comprise the worst candidate pool for teaching thoroughly alienated and disaffected young people. The school experience of successful students bears little relationship to what struggling students think and feel every day.

What are the students' commitments to learning? What is preventing young people from preparing for their futures?

Students have been trained to declare "school is important for my future." Yet, there may be a gap between that statement and what they actually demonstrate from day to day. If they don't cooperate and do the work, then their behavior expresses that they aren't convinced school matters for their lives or future.

Students initially give little permission to teachers. Young people have no control over their physical presence in the classroom. They must attend school. But real education depends on the teacher's connection to their students' minds and hearts. As with all people, those are freely given, or withheld. The teacher ought to think in terms of enlisting students' cooperation in the learning process.

It may be quite a rational assessment for a young person to withhold commitment. The education of the adults in their world may not have had much relationship to how these grown-ups have lived their lives. A few ambitious students may be willing to take the great leap of faith that schooling matters despite the abundant evidence to the contrary. But students acting on such a belief may thus imply they forsake those around them. Most human beings don't want to leave behind their family, their friends, and their community. If embracing schooling and its values means rejecting their intimate connections, young people quite sensibly refuse to do so.

What may be termed lack of commitment might therefore be regarded as cultural resistance, with its ancient roots in human consciousness. The disruptive classroom becomes the latest battleground of a struggle thousands of years old. If students view school as the work of unwelcome missionaries, no wonder teachers find themselves immersed in an alien and hostile land.

Achieving student commitment to the learning process thus becomes central to a teacher's efforts. This is a far different project than enforcing rules or discipline.

How have classroom issues been handled so far during the year?

If the teacher has expressed anger, been passive, or appeared seemingly indifferent, all these previous feelings will come to bear on what is now possible in such a classroom. If the anger, for example, was experienced by the students as disproportionate, or insulting to them, their further disruption informs the teacher of their complaint. Or, if students felt the teacher didn't care about them or their education, then their behavior might reciprocate the perceived indifference.

Teachers form a relationship over time with their students. It builds, or it doesn't, from day to day. Trust, acceptance, and tolerance occur in the accumulating interactions. As a teacher tries to ponder what's going wrong, what has happened already becomes crucial testimony toward an examination of what to do in the future.

How does the teacher feel about the students?

It is very difficult to hide contempt, particularly from the detection of those most vulnerable to the consequences of such a sentiment. Students are sharply attuned to know if the teacher thinks they're stupid, possibly even before the teacher becomes aware of feeling that way. The same holds true for any other sort of low regard. If the teacher blames the students for feeling inadequate, students will respond with their own defensiveness or animosity toward the teacher.

Teachers must begin by themselves the arduous process of working through such feelings toward students. The journey from viewing students as monsters or dolts or terrorists to appreciating them as human beings with all such complexities may at some point involve the students themselves, but mostly such efforts ought to be done inside the teacher's consciousness.

What is the material of the curriculum?

Students ought not to be blamed if the curriculum doesn't connect to them or their interests. If the school board or administration forces teachers to present material in the classroom that alienates students, or if the material is too disturbing for students, ripping them too quickly from their childhoods and its certainties, they will try their best to counterattack. A chaotic classroom might indicate the curriculum doesn't fit.

If teachers find themselves in the middle between the strictures imposed from outside the classroom, and how students react to them, they ought to value preserving the alliance with students as much as possible. At least students won't then view the teacher as the willing agent of the stultifying or insulting or irrelevant curriculum demands.

What time of the year is it?

Veteran teachers have a sense of the rhythm of a school year. Some work can't be approached until after students have settled into school and its daily labors. As was noted in the discussion of J.D. Salinger's *Catcher in the Rye* (in volume one), it made a world of difference to offer the novel in November. In September, it was too early. Students weren't focused, hadn't understood the intellectual and emotional task involved in comprehension of the novel. To grasp the sense of Holden's crippling grief required an initial two-month initiation for the students.

Throughout the year, then, a teacher needs to present material that is commensurate with students' abilities to concentrate at that particular moment. A class that requires strenuous effort ought not to be scheduled before a school holiday, like the day before Thanksgiving, or the week before winter break. Not only will there be more absentees, who will miss this important class, but students present in body will also have much more than one foot out the door. There's even a yearly peak, around March or April. After that, what with spring sports and romance and beautiful weather, the teacher can't achieve as much student focus as during fall and winter. Getting a feel for this rhythm allows teachers to avoid the difficulties of a discordance between the teacher and students in an otherwise working classroom relationship.

What are the sociological dynamics of the particular classroom?

Teachers need to be aware of all the dynamics at play in a group of students. Students are human beings with little social or political power and, frequently, little connection to their personal power. They depend for their safety and security on detecting clues in a world often quite mysterious to them. It matters greatly for their well-being to notice if a teacher favors one gender, one race, or one group of individuals. It explains why they aren't called on, or receive praise or good grades. Such tip-offs of a teacher's sentiments may evoke student anger. Teachers need to be quite careful about their praise of one group, or their admonitions toward another, lest they stir jealousy or resentment. Young people, often quite unconsciously, carry the weight of their ancestors deep in their psyches. A slight, real or imagined, to their people or their gender may evoke great passion. Students may have little understanding of this power. But a teacher wishing to maintain an effective ongoing relationship with those students must never lose sight of these dynamics.

The felt experience of helplessness in daily life for most young people causes matters of pride to assume great importance. The lives of adolescents are limited in ways that would be intolerable to adults. These factors make young people far more susceptible to shame. All this makes a teacher embarrassing students in front of their peer group deeply painful. It may cause levels of resentment and resistance teachers have little understanding of, until the teachers realize how passionately they are resented. The classroom may become a place for the shamed student to seek revenge.

Despite how wonderful it might feel to blow up, and tell off the class, have them tremble or sit quietly for days or weeks, such methods don't prove effective for education. Students may comply, even cooperate, but whatever the forces were that provoked the teacher's explosion will reassemble. Anger creates no understanding, no expression of what prompts students to disrupt or disengage. It's not effective because there's too large a power differential between a teacher and students. There's no possible reciprocity of emotion. Teachers can yell. Students can't. A teacher expressing anger only reinforces the distance between the two, creating more separation where what's needed is connection.

It may be beyond the capacity of normal human beings to maintain a long-term relationship with people without friction, lost tempers, yelling and screaming. Teachers ought not to aspire to sainthood. But expressions of anger ought to generate analysis. Somehow, someway, the fundamental unity of educational purpose is ruptured. It is up to the teacher to seek an understanding of the difficulty. Time for the teacher to ponder what is wrong, and repair the relationship. It usually involves a frank and humble apology by the teacher. The teacher should be brief, and not expect students to accept their contrition. Captive, dependent people can't freely forgive. The task is rather to remedy whatever was the issue.

This is why I once tipped over my teacher's desk, spewing papers all over the floor, and what I did about it: I was in the middle of a class lecture. Just starting to get into it, when there was the announcement that students who were on the honor roll were to report to an assembly where they would all receive ice cream. This involved at least a third of my class. It was the last straw in all sorts of ways. I resented every classroom disruption of such nature. It seemed that the administration regarded students as merely sitting in class, doing nothing of any importance, just waiting for administrators to call for them.

The announcement meant I would have to forego the rest of the class. I also thought such an assembly for honor roll students made everyone else, struggling through their school lives, feel inadequate. Awards honor those lucky enough to do school without also working a job twenty hours or more a week, or having a quiet bedroom to do homework in, or not afflicted with various emotional or cognitive maladies that beset the young. I say let the luck and the real long-term benefits of good grades be their own reward, and not rub it in the face of those less fortunate.

I had been diagnosed with prostate cancer. I was going in for surgery in a week. It took me a while to accept that my own feelings of fear and helplessness contributed to my colossal meltdown.

I told students I had behaved badly, disrupting the classroom far more than any of them had ever done. I explained that I must have been dreading, in ways I wasn't aware of, the diagnosis of and operation for cancer. I hoped that they would forgive me, and that we might get back to work. These students were a forgiving lot. Over time, we were able to reestablish a focus on classroom work. It took longer to forgive myself. I find it is easier to accept the humanity of others than I do my own. Humility is endless, says Eliot.

This incident is but one of several on my path to insight about the destructive nature of a teacher expressing anger in a classroom setting.

What practices might teachers cultivate that will enhance their ability to maintain an effective classroom environment?

Young people are actually quite conservative. So much is changing inside them, their bodies, their consciousness, their relationships with those they love, they naturally desire as much as possible to have the security of a familiar pattern of classroom activities. They derive comfort in the predictable. A teacher, by being clear, consistent, and easy to read, can calm the ocean of anxiety in which students must swim through adolescence.

Students who can enter a classroom and take the risk of being intellectually open to a new idea can do so because they aren't frightened. They know the structure of what's going to happen in the class. They can engage in the work because their surroundings are familiar and safe. As much as possible, students ought to know what the assignments are, in plenty of time; be able to anticipate the demands on their time and energy; and have a form to the class where there aren't surprises or unanticipated challenges.

A teacher needs to conduct corrective conversations with students in private. To admonish someone of much less power than the teacher in a classroom setting can set in motion forces that the teacher knows nothing about. Students exist in a complex community. Saying harsh words to this one person, witnessed by many members of this community, can reverberate in unanticipated ways. It may strengthen the resolve of all to combat the teacher. More dreadfully, it may reinforce the sense of isolation of this one student. It may be used as ammunition for taunts or rejection by the student's peers.

The concern of the teacher and students is the pursuit of knowledge, not feelings. Conversations between these two ought to focus on restoring a working relationship, not simply expressing feelings. This may seem contradictory, since much of this chapter is focused on teachers being sensitive to students' feelings. But the criterion for success isn't that everyone is happy. What matters is whether students have learned what the teacher has set out to teach. This must involve feelings, as all human endeavors ought to. But as teachers judge their success, it ought to be centered on the restoration of a teaching relationship, not on the participants' feelings.

How might a teacher resolve the conundrums involved in managing a teaching environment?

There are some conundrums that talking of classroom management evokes. Students who seem to resist the most, who are the biggest pains in the class, may be doing so because they are the ones paying attention the most. They haven't resigned themselves. They are hungry for something from the teacher or the class. To resolve the conundrum may involve the teacher transforming their negative energy into something worthwhile, for them, the class, even for the teacher. The teacher ought thus to ponder how it came about that one individual became the focus of much of the classroom disruption. The student may have been appointed, quite unconsciously but powerfully, as the designated spokesperson for the group.

In the same fashion, a teacher's frustration, anger, exhaustion, and despair may be signs of ambition, of desires to have students learn that aren't being met. Classroom order can be maintained thoroughly if submission is the chief goal. A teacher needs only to make it so painful for students to step out of line that they sit quietly because there's less agony in that option compared to the others. A seemingly well-ordered classroom may be a gathering of frightened people. Only an ambitious teacher would inquire about what gets learned in such an environment. Constant struggle to enlist students' consent and cooperation in learning may be far more arduous and difficult, and leave an ambitious teacher exhausted.

Perhaps the biggest conundrum involves the receptivity to new ideas, which may spring from disorder and messiness just as much as from seeming harmony. By high school, students have had to develop techniques to get themselves through the day, through the year, with minimal damage to their sense of well-being. They've been forced to adapt to numerous adults coming at them with their demands, sometimes with insults, threats, or rage. Students' masks protect their privacy, to preserve for themselves how they really think and feel. To resolve the conundrum of the students' masks, teachers ought not to think in terms of domination of these individuals. Rather, a teacher should strive to achieve a negotiated relationship with them that respects their integrity. Students may be willing to come out from behind their masks if they get to choose whether they will commit to the learning process or not.

A quick glance from an administrator or visitor to the classroom can't discern whether students are listening or merely pretending to listen; thinking or merely sitting quietly; being open to a new idea, or merely hiding behind a mask. Real learning represents an internal process, not something visible.

What can be done about a disturbed and disturbing student in a classroom setting?

Despite much examination by the teacher of classroom practice and policies, especially the dynamics of how one student sometimes speaks for the group, some few students may demonstrate they are unable to connect to the teacher or the learning process. They may be too angry, too unmoored, too far beyond the teacher's ability to include them in the classroom functions. What to do?

First, of course, ought to come the teacher posing the question, why are the students getting in their own way? These young persons aren't preparing for their life. Next ought to come compassion for such persons, caught in some frame of mind, some unexamined or unknown behavior pattern, that causes them and others such pain or works at such cross-purposes for their own welfare.

Anger at such troubled persons is particularly deleterious. The teacher ought to exercise even greater care than usual to contain such feelings engendered by the teacher's helplessness or frustration. A teacher must understand that such individuals are trapped inside themselves, with no words, perhaps no understanding of themselves. They are beset of mind and spirit.

Within the bounds of respect for the young person's privacy, Everyone in the school community needs to be involved in the conversation about such a beleaguered student. This includes other teachers, parents, grandparents, neighbors, school administrators, and psychologists. The understanding of psychology and mental illness isn't very advanced compared to what science knows in physics, chemistry, and biology. Much progress is being made on why people harm themselves, but diagnosis and treatment remain hunches, guesswork, trial and error. Sometimes proper medication is useful. Sometimes psychotherapy is. Everything ought to be tried, all resources mobilized.

The sooner a troubled young person gets help, the better off the individual, the classroom, and society will be. Teachers are often the first to notice and sound the alarm. Whatever energy can be called forth, to assist a young person in such dire straits, ought to be employed.

In sum

Classroom management embodies a delicate and perplexing art. In this regard, it resembles all human relationships, particularly those organized to complete a task. The teacher must understand that he or she constitutes the only person in the room, at least initially, who has committed himself or herself of his or her own free will to the educational effort. Students and teachers relating to one another incorporate the dynamics of the society and the community and the ages. When done well, classroom management looks easy, merging into the mystery and serendipity of good marriages, successful parenting, the synergies of creative partnerships. When done poorly, nothing else can take place. But an aware and reflective and humble teacher can witness and adjust, as William Carlos Williams suggests.[1]

NOTE

1. In his poem, "To Elsie," about a mentally impaired young woman, Williams characterized her isolation as "No one to witness and adjust, no one to drive the car."

Chapter 30

Teachers, Students, and Mental Illness

Someone who has read about Holden Caulfield in volume one, or the discussion of the essays by Andrew Solomon and Kay Jamison, along with Herman Melville's "Bartleby the Scrivener," and the consideration of Septimus Smith in Virginia Woolf's *Mrs. Dalloway* in this volume's chapter 17, will have a sense of this book's perspective on mental illness. There has also been a brief look at teachers contending with a student's affliction in chapter 26's talk of "pushy parents," and the previous chapter's talk of disturbing students.

Some might hold that all teenagers are mentally ill. Young people's impulsiveness, their vast indifference to danger, their recklessness with matters of the heart, their newness to sexual feelings and their yearnings and devastations, may cause a dispassionate observer to believe all of them have lost their minds. Despair abounds as an ambitious young person's desire for achievement becomes overmatched by the inherent limitations of time, energy, or talent. The anguish of failure plagues the lives of such people, in ways that in five or ten years will be regarded with rueful humor. The myopia of young persons, indifferent to the relationship between their actions now and preparation for an economic future, might seem pathological.

Adolescence is a different sort of human consciousness, as is traveling to a land with strange customs, or assuming any new role in life, without the comforting references or familiarity with change and adjustment. So, yes, compassion for all humans caught in such a state of life is in order.

But people depressed or withdrawn into themselves, like Melville's Bartleby, or desperate and delusional like Woolf's Septimus Smith, struggle against far more profound difficulties than those faced by adolescents. It isn't so much that their pain is greater. It may be. But the illness might actually insulate them from agony. The affliction does inhibit the learning, the living, the process of growing up. It isolates the sufferers, cutting them off from others, from themselves and their desires. Illness blocks vitality.

But building on the point of view from previous chapters, here the focus will be directly on how teachers might understand and relate to students afflicted with mental illness.

Teachers have much opportunity to engage with troubled students. Teachers end up knowing more young people than school administrators, social workers, and psychotherapists, and in ways that even parents usually don't. In both the constant contact of a classroom, or in the communications available through written work, students reveal themselves to teachers. A teacher thus has the opportunity to become the first adult to whom a young person might indicate he or she is afflicted.

As has been said before, in their course policies, teachers ought to relate to a student's depression, anxiety, or other crippling emotional or mental states as if the student had mononucleosis or a broken leg, or a severe physical illness that might require rehabilitation therapy. However a teacher adjusts grades or assignments for missing classes, or work not done, that would apply for physical maladies, ought to be used for psychological ones. Teachers must understand that afflicted students can't concentrate very much or very well. That may be the very definition of a troubled mind. The illness occupies consciousness, crowding out a focus on the concerns of a student's present life. Teachers must accept, as Andrew Solomon writes, that a person's willpower has little ability to overcome the virulence of mental illness.

Bartleby couldn't change. It wasn't a matter of how hard he tried. The narrator's insight, in the last lines, "Ah, Bartleby, ah, humanity," expresses the compassion of a witness to the devastation caused by mental illness. It cripples Bartleby's ability to connect with others. He couldn't permit someone to help him. Despite having plentiful food to eat, Bartleby starves to death.

Bartleby, scorned by his co-workers, abandoned by his employer, evokes in them the feelings toward The Other. Despite a conviction that everyone is a human being, or, in the narrator's Christian formulation, a child of God, they find it difficult to accept Bartleby's humanity. Mentally ill people so quickly can emerge as monsters in the imagination of those around them.

Holden Caulfield himself, without an observer knowing his brother Allie had died, might seem to be mentally ill. His portrayal demonstrates how close the line is between a person in anguish because of terrible loss and someone afflicted. Mental illness itself might be thought of as human emotion without a discernable cause. That's why a necessary element for contending with students who seem to be ill would be a teacher's curiosity. An understanding of his grief at his brother's death explains why Holden is unable to attend to his ongoing life. Similarly, a young person who comes to class drunk or stoned may not simply be a goofball. Such behavior may indicate someone learning how to use readily available chemical substances to mask or self-treat mental illness. A teacher might thus become the first adult to begin to pose important questions to the student.

Teachers, in dealing with the afflicted, ought to take a perspective similar to that of the medical profession. A teacher's policies and procedures should seek to do no further harm. There shouldn't be academic stress on someone struggling to contend with affliction.

Young people, suddenly beset with mental illness, typically feel much despair. Having inculcated the notion of the critical relationship of high school to their future, they dread an illness might wreck it all. A teacher ought to be careful not to make such fears rational. While teachers want students to apply themselves with a sense of meaning and purpose toward preparing for their futures, a student will have many chances to build a life. There's no rush or urgency, even if the path of recovery takes years. A teacher's behavior with an afflicted person might show how despair, like anger, fear, jealousy, or any other emotion, comes and goes. Despair possesses no more reality or permanence than any other emotion.

While teachers might be a source of information, comfort, and support for an afflicted student, they must understand they can't rescue, or cure, or save a young person. For one thing, the teacher isn't equipped by training to do so, any more than if the student had a heart ailment. Teachers are limited by their professional focus on the mind, not the psyche. They labor to have the young learn. Care of an ill psyche isn't a cognitive function. It is more akin to skill development rather than something imparted from a book or an idea. Teachers, like the narrator in Bartleby, must accept that such care of the soul isn't something they are trained for.

Teachers don't have the emotional or psychological distance that a psychotherapist would have, that permits clarity of judgment to prevail over the promptings of the heart. While this may be pointing out the obvious, such clear-sightedness can get obscured in the urgency generated by an ill student. This is particularly true when the teachers see much of themselves or their own struggles in the afflicted student. Then the urge to be a catcher in the rye, saving other children since the first child was lost, can overwhelm good judgment.

What a teacher can do is convince the student that a team effort is needed. The student needs help. There are professionals who do this work. It isn't the time for people to cut themselves off from the care of loved ones. As with other aspects of teacher and student interactions discussed in this book, the teacher's first efforts ought to be to enlist the students' cooperation in contending with their illness. The students' shame that they are afflicted can cause them to feel isolated. A teacher ought not to compound that isolation by making the students feel betrayed by the teacher's divulging information given in confidence. Sometimes, students may be so out of touch with themselves or the seriousness of the state of their illness that a teacher may need to talk to others without the student's permission. But such an act carries the risk of damaging or destroying the intimacy the teacher enjoys with the student.

Part of the difficulty of relating to mentally ill people is that they evoke the irrationality of those around them. Consider how Bartleby's co-workers started saying "I prefer not" as if they had been infected by Bartleby's refusals. Depressed people make others sad. Raging people make others angry. Anxious people make others nervous. It is difficult to keep clear boundaries between one psyche and another. Teachers seeking to aid an afflicted student might find themselves drawn into the student's world, instead of helping to extract the student from it.

Teachers ought to keep in mind that they will receive little recognition or gratitude from an afflicted person, even after an episode ends. The student might return kindness with abuse, assistance with blame. Part of what makes helping someone with mental illness so difficult is that it isn't very rewarding, as Bartleby's narrator found out. Mental illness occludes the vision of sufferers as they regard those who try to assist them.

Sometimes there's nothing to be done. To connect with someone suffering from mental illness may mean to be involved in events beyond anyone's control. A person who cares for someone beset may only experience helplessness. But this would be true if the teacher were involved in any of the terrible events that might befall the young: deaths from car crashes, alcohol poisonings, ski accidents, murders arising from jealousy or rage, fatal illnesses. To be a teacher means to be involved in the vicissitudes of the lives of others, its triumphs and tragedies.

Appendix 1

Senior Class Essay Topics

12AP-EA-1: Due Aug. 31. Write a 750-word essay, formatted in compliance with the essay stipulations listed on page 4 of the Syllabus, about the following topic. How do you intend to think and respond to the awareness of your own privilege?

12AP-EA-2: Due Sept. 9. Write a 750-word essay about the following topic. What is your attitude toward substances such as narcotics and alcohol, that change consciousness? Does your behavior correspond to this attitude?

12AP-EA-3: Due Sept. 20. Write a 750-word essay where you connect to some aspect of the portrayal of Pip or some other character in *Great Expectations*. Talk about how this portrayal resonates in your own life.

12AP-EA-4: Due Sept. 28. Write a 750-word essay where you offer some observations about how a historical event influenced the life of some loved one.

12AP-EA-5: Due Oct. 8. Write a 750-word essay where you consider the moral implications that might be derived from the historical research Alperowitz offers in the selections from his *The Decision to Drop the Atomic Bomb*.

12AP-EA-6: Due Oct. 15. Write a 750-word essay where you offer an expression of what you hold as a matter of faith.

12AP-EA-7: Due Oct. 22. Write a 750-word essay where you ponder what you know about homophobia.

12AP-EA-8: Due Nov. 4. Write a 1000-word essay where you offer observations about the English language. You may comment on its idioms, its constructions, its dialects, its slang, its baffling absurdity (consider explaining what the word *fly* means). You may discuss the words that have the most meaning and power in your life.

12AP-EA-9: Due Nov. 19. Write a 1000-word essay where you take Jonathan Lear's analysis from his *Radical Hope*, and apply it to some contemporary human struggle, from the Israeli-Palestinian conflict, to India and Pakistan over Kashmir, to immigration struggles in the United States, to conflict over the removal of Roma (Gypsy) settlements in European nations. (Note: if you choose other conflicts, check with me before you do so for approval.)

12AP-EA-10: Due Dec. 3: Write a 1000-word essay where you compare and contrast Hamlet's struggle with your own class, culture, or parental struggles.

12AP-EA-11: Due Dec. 15: Write a 1000-word essay where you attempt to dissolve the distance between you and Raskolnikov.

12AP-EA-12: Due Jan. 10. Get from me an AP exam question from a previous year. Spend no more than 40 minutes on it. This will not be able to be revised.

12AP-EA-13: Done in class on Jan. 18, a 40-minute AP exam question from a previous year.

12AP-EA-14: Due Jan. 24. Go to the website TED.com. Search the various talks, until you find one that is interesting to you. It must be over 20 minutes long. Listen to it a couple times. Then write a 1000-word essay, where you briefly summarize (150 words) the speaker's ideas, then offer your own thinking about what the speaker has said.

12AP-EA-15: Due Feb. 7. In 1000 words, offer some thinking about the reverberations of *Frankenstein* in modern culture.

12AP-EA-16: Due Feb. 23. In 1000 words, consider some aspect of the warrior culture or myth in American consciousness.

12AP-EA-17: Due March 8. In 1000 words, describe how the image or spirit of Don Quixote manifests itself in our culture.

12AP-EA-18: Due March 16. Get from me an AP exam question from a previous year. Spend no more than 40 minutes on it.

[EA-19 through 21 the same as EA-18]

12AP-EA-22: Due May 27. In 2000 words, select four works discussed in class (the list is on the back of this sheet). One must be a novel, the second a poem, the third must be either a nonfiction book or a short story, and the fourth must be a play. In about 500 words each, discuss these works around one of the possible topics listed below. Other topics may be used with my approval. This essay will not be able to be revised, but drafts, of any length, can be submitted in advance of the due date for my comments.

1. Art is the portrayal of the struggle for human rights.
2. My thinking has changed or deepened by considering these four works.
3. Literary artists are immersed in history.
4. Literary analysis helps us uncover the truth of the human experience.

Appendix 2

Syllabus

THEMES OF THIS COURSE

This class will use some classical and contemporary literature to inquire into questions raised by moral philosophy, psychology, and contemporary literary theory. The countries of origin of the texts will range from America to Russia to Israel and Palestine, but the focus will mainly be on literature from the British Isles.

We will seek to understand good action. Our study will encompass issues of human rights, as well as the portrayal of human suffering caused by oppression. We will ponder the mentality of murderers like Raskolnikov, Sethe, Hamlet, Dorian Gray, Dr. Frankenstein, Oedipus, and Medea. We will use literature to gain a deeper understanding of the struggles of romance. We will examine the nature and dynamics of belief.

TEXTS NEEDED

I will provide essays, most plays, short stories, and poems. You will be expected to furnish all novels, Shakespeare plays, and works of nonfiction. Some novels must be read in the specified translation. They are available at Politics and Prose bookstore, 5015 Connecticut Ave. NW, Washington, DC, 202-364-1919.

READING LIST

FIRST ADVISORY: (August, September, October)

Novels: *Great Expectations,* Charles Dickens
The Plague, Albert Camus
The Picture of Dorian Gray, Oscar Wilde

Poets: Seamus Heaney, Bertolt Brecht, William Blake

Plays: *Oedipus the King* (Fagles translation), Sophocles
The Bacchae (David Greig translation), Euripedes

Short Story: "Brokeback Mountain," Annie Proulx

Nonfiction: *Strength in What Remains,* Tracy Kidder

Essays: "What Are You Going to Do with That?" by Mark Danner; "What Have We Learned, If Anything?" by Tony Judt; "Euphemism and American Violence" by David Bromwich; "If We Fail to Act" by Paul Farmer; "Holocaust: The Ignored Reality" by Timothy Snyder; selections from *The Decision to Drop the Atomic Bomb* by Gar Alperovitz; selections from *Homosexuality and Civilization* by Louis Crompton

SECOND ADVISORY: (November, December, January)

Novels: *Crime and Punishment,* Fyodor Dostoevsky (translated by Pevear and Volokhonsky)
Beloved, Toni Morrison
Mrs. Dalloway, Virginia Woolf

Poets: Anna Akhmatova, William Wordsworth, Eavan Boland, T. S. Eliot, Samuel Taylor Coleridge

Plays: *The Importance of Being Earnest,* Oscar Wilde
Hamlet, William Shakespeare

Essays: "Hannah Arendt," Samantha Power; "First Loves," Michael Igna-
          tieff; review and selections from *Radical Hope, Ethics in the Face
          of Cultural Devastation* by Jonathan Lear; review and selections
          from *Once Upon a Country: A Palestinian Life* by Sari Nusseibeh;
          "Vengeance Is Ours" by Jared Diamond

THIRD ADVISORY: (February, March, April)

Novels: *Frankenstein* (1818 Text) by Mary Shelley
          Selections from *Don Quixote,* Miguel de Cervantes
          Beowulf, translated by Seamus Heaney

Poets: Komachi/Shikibu, William Butler Yeats, Wisława Szymborska,
          Percy Bysshe Shelley, Robert Browning, Matthew Arnold

Plays: *Romeo and Juliet,* William Shakespeare
          Copenhagen, Michael Frayen
          Rosencrantz and Guildenstern Are Dead, Tom Stoppard
          Richard III, William Shakespeare

Essays: "Imagining the Worst," Tom Reiss; "Yeats/Larkin," Seamus
          Heaney; "What Really Happened at Copenhagen?" Thomas Pow-
          ers (and related pieces); "The Hunger Warriors," Scott Anderson;
          "The Imitation of Our Lord Don Quixote," Geoffrey O'Brien

FOURTH ADVISORY: (May)

Poets: John Donne, Geoffrey Chaucer

Plays: *The Caucasian Chalk Circle,* Bertolt Brecht
          King Lear, William Shakespeare

AP CREDIT OR GRADE-LEVEL CREDIT

In order to receive AP credit (weighted) for this class, students must take the
AP exam in May. Students who elect not to take the exam will receive regular
credit for the course.

GRADES

Advanced Placement courses are considered college level courses. Students who score a 3 or better on the AP exam in May are eligible for credit at many colleges and universities, or exempted from typical first-year college English survey courses. Grading criteria for this course will reflect this higher level.

Criteria for assigned essays:

A — if the writing possesses many of the following attributes: clarity, thoughtfulness, good organization, logical development of ideas, vividness, fresh and lively prose. It also must be free of grammatical or mechanical errors, and comprehensively cover the topic assigned.

B — if the writing does not possess many of the attributes of an **A** paper, but is free of mechanical errors, and covers decently the topic assigned.

C — if the writing is free of mechanical errors, but possesses few of the attributes of an **A** paper.

zero — if no essay is submitted.

[Typically, no grade lower than a **C plus** will be given. Essays that don't qualify for at least a **C plus** will be required to be done over.]

Deadlines for assigned essays: Students who are interested in a good grade for this course typically submit their assigned essays on the date stipulated in the lesson plan. There's so much volume that postponing submission of an essay only serves to create a vortex of debt. If late submissions become a chronic issue with a student, I may choose to provide an additional incentive by invoking the following penalty: if an assigned essay is submitted more than twenty-four hours after the due date listed in the lesson plan, no grade higher than a B for first submission may be given. If it is submitted forty-eight hours after the due date, no grade higher than a C may be given initially. Essays over two weeks late may not be revised for a grade higher than a C.

TESTS

Essay tests, taken in class, measure students' ability to comprehend and write clearly about the text and an analysis of it. Students who read the literature before the class discussion, pay attention and take notes during the class, and then review the assigned work and their notes before the test, should be well prepared for these tests. Students are permitted to use texts and their own class notes during the essay ("Part 2") tests. Review sessions before these essay tests are available for all students, at lunchtime, by request.

At the beginning of the first class where a text is to be discussed, an initial, short answer quiz ("Part 1") will be given. It will consist of five to ten questions worth one or two points each. Students will not be permitted to use their texts, or notes, to take these initial Part 1 tests. The essay test is Part 2. All tests, both Part 1 and Part 2, will be announced in advance in the lesson plans.

If a student cannot attend a class when a Part 1 test is being given, make-up tests will be given at the time of the essay test for that material. No make-up tests will be given other than at this time. Part 2 (essay test) make-up tests for students who miss the test will be given at lunchtime, for only the following week.

For Part 2 essay tests, each test question is assigned a point value at the top of the test. Grading is based on that value, or fractions of that value for less than complete answers. Correct answers may be discussed in class when the corrected tests are returned. Part 2 tests typically consist of two parts: Section One questions require a paragraph or two to be answered properly; Section Two consists of a choice of one of three essay questions.

ADVISORY GRADING VALUES

For the first three advisories, assigned essays account for 60 percentage of advisory grades and tests for 40 percentage; grading values during the Fourth Advisory will be 15 percentage for short essays; 25 percentage for essay tests; and 60 percentage for the longer essay.

All replies to grade status inquiries will be in writing. No "incompletes" for advisory grades will be given. Except for proven errors on the part of the teacher, all advisory grades are final. No make-up work, after the end of the advisory, will be accepted. It is each student's responsibility to ascertain grade status before the end of each grading period.

COURSE WORK EXPECTATIONS

Periodically (typically, once per month), a lesson plan will be given out in class, covering assignments due. It will include reading assignments, essays due during that time, and all tests scheduled. Students are responsible for getting a lesson plan, if they miss the class where it is handed out.

There will be four essays, of 1000 to 1500 words in length, assigned every advisory. One longer written work, of 2500 words, will be due in the Fourth Advisory.

Assigned essays must conform to the Assigned Essay Stipulations (page 4). Revised essays must conform to the Revised Essay Stipulations. Students are obligated to retain all work handed back, both essay tests and assigned essays. An essay assignment during the year may require students to use these returned assignments. In cases where a student claims to have done work where there is no grade recorded, the only proof accepted for having done the work is the returned, graded work itself.

CLASS MEMBERSHIP POLICY

This is intended to be an intellectually rigorous class that will demand a fair amount of a student's time and energy. Students who make the effort will pass. Most school days, I will be available at lunchtime for student questions, comments, and concerns.

Email submissions: Students may use email to communicate questions about assignments, but assigned essays must be submitted in hard copy. Assigned essays may not be emailed.

ESSAY STIPULATIONS: Essays will not be read or graded unless these stipulations are followed:

1. All assigned essays must be word processed, in 10-point type, standard fonts (such as Times Roman, Arial, Courier). No other character fonts or point type will be accepted. Essays must be single spaced, with two-inch margins. 1000-word essays should be on two pages, 1500-word essays on three pages.
2. In the upper right-hand corner must appear only class, the assignment number, including topic number, and the word count of the essay. The essay should then follow. [There should be no date, essay topic title, student name, explanations or other marginalia.] See sample below.
3. Word count must be within 5 percentage of the assigned length. For a 1000-word essay, this means between 950 and 1050 words, and for a 1500-word essay, 1425 to 1575 words.
4. The student identification number should appear on the back of the last page of the essay. There should be no other identifying marks on the essay.
5. Assigned essays must contain the student's own thinking and wording. If the student consults any literary or scholarly works, or has discussions with fellow students or others, this must be noted in parentheses at the end of the essay. There will be no grade penalty for such attributions. Every student is responsible for protecting the integrity of his or her work from others who might wish to submit it as their own.

6. Discrepancies between the real and stated word count will result in a failed grade for that assignment.
7. All assigned essays submitted on time, except AP exam questions, are eligible for a revised grade upon resubmission (see revision stipulations below).
8. Essays with more than an occasional mechanical error (grammar, homonyms, misspelling, punctuation) will be returned ungraded. The essay must be revised and resubmitted, free of all mechanical errors, not just the ones pointed out, in order to receive a grade.

STIPULATIONS FOR ESSAY REVISIONS

1. Students must respond to all teacher comments about their original submission. This may be done by numbering all teacher comments, and listing the responses. It may also be done in an essay response.
2. Total word length of the revision must be between 25 percentage and 40 percentage of the original essay word length.
3. The essay revision must be submitted on top of the copy of the original essay that has teacher comments.
4. Revised essays may be submitted for a higher grade only once.
5. Revised essays are due one week after they have been returned to the student.

Appendix 3

Some Works Put Aside

Over the years there have been several works tried that were then taken off the syllabus. To talk about why they were put aside might indicate some of the thinking that guided the selection of works throughout the course. While recognizing that much more may be said about all the issues involved, the rationale offered here will be brief.

In these high school courses, where the effort was to acquaint students with a broad perspective on either American or British/Continental literature, sometimes works were well received, but didn't continue in the curriculum. They took time away from covering other areas of literature. Building a curriculum for a survey course involves making difficult choices. Although arguments may be made against the notion of a survey course itself, the courses of this book intended to provide such an overview of literature to students.

WHITE TEETH BY ZADIE SMITH

Amazing first novel by a very young British-Pakistani woman. It's full of humor, romance, intrigue, the difficulties of the contemporary immigrant experience, particularly for people from Muslim countries. The novel shows how young people inherit the rage of oppression from their previous generations, causing them to do terrible things. Students responded well to it. Class discussions about it were energetic and thoughtful. It worked well as an opening novel for the senior class.

As it became clearer and clearer how the senior course was far more constricted than the junior course because of senioritis (see chapter 20 of Volume Two), it meant choosing between this good contemporary novel and Charles Dickens' *Great Expectations*. That was the slot in the course structure for one or the other. While the course reflects ambivalence about the canon, it places importance on students having a sense of the literary tradition. Thus it seemed more important for students to engage with Dickens' novel. Students might, on their own, come across Zadie Smith's work. Far fewer would pick up Dickens.

This is all rather slight reasoning. But such are the difficulties when there are so many books, and so little time.

"AFTER THE GENOCIDE" BY PHILIP GOUREVITCH

This essay from *The New Yorker,* a report about the Rwandan genocide, was used for a couple of years as a lead up to the study of Albert Camus' *The Plague.* The intent was to introduce a contemporary instance of horror to connect to Camus' thinking about WWII. In light of the continuing evil in the world, how might Camus' statement at the end of his novel, *there is more to admire in humanity than despise,* be understood?

It was too much for students. They couldn't achieve any distance to ponder these intellectual or moral issues. Substituting Tracy Kidder's *Strength in What Remains*, which tells of a young man escaping the genocide in his country and making his way to the United States (chapter 6 of Volume Two), while touching only briefly on the events that made him flee, proved to be effective at bringing the issue of contemporary genocide into the course.

THE SORROW OF WAR BY BAO NINH

SAMSKARA, A RITE FOR A DEAD MAN
BY U. R. ANANTHA MURTHY

These two novels present fascinating other worlds for students to consider. Ninh's book portrays two lovers from North Vietnam, caught up in (what they called) The Great Patriotic War against the Americans. It tells of the terrible destruction of that war, from the perspective of the people that won, at the cost of three million of their countrymen.

It's also something of a love story, albeit not a very happy one, since the characters are so overwhelmed by the horror of the war. There's too much death for life or love to find expression. As in Morrison's *Beloved,* these people will need much time and safety to overcome the shock from all the suffering they've endured.

Murthy's novel tells of a spiritual crisis of a holy man in a remote Indian village in the middle of the twentieth century. His opposite, a sinner who renounces his Brahmin faith and culture, has died. The holy man must consider whether the burial ought to be done according to the customs of his faith. He decides not to administer the rituals. He sleeps with the dead man's low-caste mistress, and ends up losing his own faith. But this carries with it the potential for his own personal liberation.

Had the entire course been built around Camus' *The Plague,* it might have been quite useful in deepening different aspects of his work. From vastly different cultures, these two novels present perspectives that evoke a sense of common humanity and its struggles. But similar to *White Teeth,* there wasn't the space in this survey course to allow these works to continue to be considered.

SWANN'S WAY (FIRST VOLUME OF *A REMEMBRANCE OF THINGS PAST*) BY MARCEL PROUST

It seemed worthwhile to give this Great One a chance, to see if some percentage of students might catch some glimpses of its brilliance. It is a story of vast yearning, intrigue, and romance. It proved to be well beyond even the best students. A few years later, one of them remarked to me that he had recently read it and enjoyed it greatly. "At the time I was just too young, I guess, to appreciate all that psychology and confusion. I do now, though."

Thus gets illustrated the notion of intellectual maturity. It does limit what students in high school can find interesting to think about. Building a curriculum for young people involves developing a sense of where there is capacity to push, and where there isn't. With Proust's masterpiece, from the one time it was assigned to students, it was clear that his work would have to wait upon their arrival down the road.

Index

About the Author

Joseph F. Riener has been involved with education and its issues for a lifetime. He most recently taught AP English at a large urban high school for 17 years.